UNSHAKEABLE:

20 WAYS TO ENJOY TEACHING EVERY DAY...NO MATTER WHAT

Also by Angela Watson

*The Cornerstone: Classroom Management That Makes Teaching
More Effective, Efficient, and Enjoyable*

Awakened: Change Your Mindset to Transform Your Teaching

The Awakened Devotional Study Guide for Christian Educators

UNSHAKEABLE:

20 WAYS TO ENJOY TEACHING EVERY DAY...NO MATTER WHAT

ANGELA WATSON

Unshakeable: 20 Ways to Enjoy Teaching Every Day...No Matter What
by Angela Watson

Copyright © 2015 by Angela Watson

Published by Due Season Press and Educational Services.

ISBN-13: 978-0-9823127-3-5
ISBN-10: 0-9823127-3-3

Table of Contents

Preface:

Can anyone really enjoy *every* day in the classroom?

I am a teacher, and I always will be, even though I'm not teaching little kids anymore.

I taught pre-kindergarten, 2nd, and 3rd grades for eleven years in the Washington, D.C., area and South Florida. After getting married and relocating to New York City in 2009 so I could be with my new husband, I found myself job hunting during the recession. During that long period of massive teacher layoffs, I jumped at the chance to do part-time work as an instructional coach in the Bronx...and I discovered that teaching other teachers could be just as rewarding for me as teaching children.

I never had the benefit of a coach or formal mentor program when I was in the classroom. I desperately needed the support of someone who understood the daily struggles of teaching, but had time to help me without needing to rush back to his or her own students.

I now have the privilege of being that person, and the support and encouragement of teachers is my top focus. My work has expanded to a wide range of tasks and services that support this mission. I write blog posts and books for teachers. I've gotten to produce a podcast, online courses, professional development workshops, and instructional coaching sessions that empower other educators. I'm a teacher of teachers, and I'm humbled when I think of how many students I'm now able to impact through this work.

A few years ago, my teaching experience was limited mostly to my own four classroom walls: now I get to visit teachers and schools all over the country. I get to spend time talking with teachers in small rural schools, and problem solve with those in big urban districts. I work with high school teachers all the way down to PreK. I feel like I have a better understanding now of what it's like to be a teacher because I get to spend more time than ever *listening to actual teachers* instead of being isolated in my own classroom.

I'm also able to spend a lot more time thinking about the big picture in education, and I'm realizing that the decision makers in our field aren't talking enough about how to tap into what makes teaching inherently rewarding. I want to see more conversations about meeting the needs of the whole teacher, more consideration of how school policies contribute to or detract from teacher motivation, and more realistic advice on how teachers can uncover a passion for their work and ignite that same passion in students.

My hope is to spark some of those conversations through this book. I can't change ridiculous school policies, reform standardized testing, reduce class sizes, or make any of the other systemic changes that would help teaching feel less insurmountable. But I *can* share practical resources that make the day-to-day stuff a little less frustrating and little more rewarding.

If I can give you some ideas for making a connection with that seemingly unreachable kid or shaving 20 minutes off a mundane task so you can focus on something more meaningful, then I feel like in some small way, I've made a difference. I've helped you keep a smile on your face for your students and end the school day on a higher note than if you hadn't read my words.

The number one goal of my work is to share strategies that make teaching not only more effective and efficient, but also *enjoyable*. And for most us, learning to enjoy our daily work will be a lifelong journey. It's not much different from making healthy food choices, or fitting exercise into a busy schedule, or prioritizing a good night's sleep. I don't know anyone who succeeds 100% in all of those areas every single day.

But each time we turn our awareness to these things—when we look around at all of our options and *choose* good health, rest, and mindful enjoyment in that moment—we move closer to the goal. When you continually make a series of small positive choices, they eventually become strong, unshakeable habits that are an essential part of who you are.

You certainly don't need another voice (inside or outside of your head) saying that you're doing things the wrong way and need to change. I encourage you to be open to the ideas in this book knowing that you won't be able to fully embody or fulfill them on a daily basis, especially not at first...and that's okay. You should also know that not every suggestion is going to be a match for your teaching style, personality, students, and district requirements.

My objective is simply to help you become more aware of a variety of positive habits and practices. That way, you can choose the ones that fit with your teaching context and incorporate them with increasing frequency until they become part of your new way of living and working.

Some days the joy will flow naturally. Other days you will have to remind yourself consciously of the principles you've learned, and force yourself to practice habits you're trying to ingrain. There will always be better days and worse days. But over time, you can create a lifestyle in which you experience more highs than lows. You can spend more time at the peaks, and not descend quite so low into the valleys.

The goal we keep striving for is to become unshakeable: so resolute in our determination to enjoy our work that no outside circumstance can steal that joy away. We can choose our mindset, choose our actions and reactions, choose to create a fun and positive learning environment in our classrooms, and choose to love teaching every day…no matter what.

Angela
March 2015

1

Share your authentic self to bring passion and energy to your teaching

Good teaching is part science and part art. There are proven best practices, but there is no one right way to teach. And it's not just your philosophy as a teacher that affects what happens in your classroom—your *personality* has a tremendous impact on the types of lessons you create, your instructional delivery, and your rapport with students.

Though teaching methods are being increasingly standardized and there is a definite movement to deny the individual teacher's role in the learning process, I would argue that *who you are as a person* is at the crux of your effectiveness. The unique personality traits, quirks, and interests you bring to the classroom can—and should—be integrated and celebrated. Your uniqueness as a human being is part of what makes your instruction interesting and creates an inviting place for students to learn.

Balance the "acting" with an integration of your authentic self

It's been said that the best teachers are also actors, and I believe that is true to a large extent. We have to act excited about teaching a lesson when we feel completely drained. We have to act enthusiastic about small measures of kids' progress when we feel frustrated that they haven't made larger gains. We have to act like we're calm and in control when we feel like screaming. Sometimes we even have to act like we believe in what we're doing when we feel like it's a waste of time.

All of that acting is done for the benefit of our students. It's not necessarily a bad thing. However, it can leave you feeling very disconnected from your true self. You may feel relieved to "get off the stage" at the end of the day and be yourself again.

One way you can combat this feeling is to bring as many elements of your true self into the classroom as possible. Let your personality shine through in the way you decorate and organize your classroom, the way you teach, and the way you interact with students.

The real you is memorable

Have you ever run into a student at the grocery store, park, or mall? If so, I'm sure you've seen the deer-caught-in-headlights stare as she or he tries to process the reality that you have a life apart from teaching: *What's she wearing? What's she buying? Who is she with?* Kids remember those moments of seeing the real you and are fascinated by them.

Those moments when your real life and interests are visible in the classroom are memorable, too. I'll never forget an American history teacher I had in high school, whom I'll call Mr. Washington. He always lectured for the entire period in a dull, monotone voice...except for the week he taught us about the assassination of John F. Kennedy. His eyes lit up for the first time all year. He had passion in his voice. He raced around the front of the room as he talked, drawing furious sketches of an iceberg on the chalkboard, pointing to the tip of it above the water and shouting, "This is the part we know about JFK!"

That was the real Mr. Washington. It was fascinating to see him excited and hear about the personal research he'd done. I can't say that his passion for history necessarily transferred to all his students, but *we remembered what he taught*. We stayed awake in class that week and actually paid attention.

Recently when my former classmates planned our high school reunion, they chose a photo of an iceberg as the header image for our Facebook group. Twenty years had passed, and every single one of us could still recall the time we saw Mr. Washington really come alive in the classroom. His teaching self—that is, the persona he had created for the classroom—was boring. But the real him was memorable.

Who you are inside—your real and authentic self—is one of the most powerful tools you have to make your lessons stick with students and help them learn. You can be the determining factor in whether the *content* you teach is memorable simply by giving kids a glimpse of the *person* you are inside. Let them see the real you, and watch as they are drawn in and make connections in new ways.

Build rapport by sharing who you are on a personal level

My former co-worker Kara has a playful personality and presents her real and silly self on pretty much all occasions. Her students know her favorite foods, colors, and flowers. They often bring her little gifts that reflect those preferences: a bar of chocolate on her birthday or a fistful of pink wildflowers pulled up from the side of

the road. She shows students pictures of things she did over the
weekend and updates them on family happenings. She laughs at her
own mistakes all the time and uses those shortcomings to create
"inside jokes" with her kids.

This type of sharing results in a tremendously strong bond
between students and the teacher. When kids feel like you are really
transparent with them, they will respond in kind. They will see you
as more than just a tyrant who enforces rules, or an omnipotent
leader who is the sole bearer of knowledge: you become *human* in
their eyes, another learner in the classroom.

I'll admit that sharing my life and personality with students
doesn't come naturally to me. I tend to be guarded and private. I fear
exposing aspects of myself that could derail our lesson, or worse,
later be used against me. But when I look back on my least
rewarding days of teaching—those days when I simply dragged
through, counting down the minutes until it was over—I realize
those were the days when I was just The Teacher instead of my
whole self. I was Mrs. Watson, but I was not Angela.

The days when I left Angela out of the classroom and only
showed Mrs. Watson were boring and forced for me, and I imagine
they felt that way for my students, too. I noticed the way that my
daydreamers suddenly perked up if I told them a story about myself
when I was their age. I saw how the entire class would sit at rapt
attention whenever I answered a question about where I'd bought
the necklace I was wearing, or what I was going to eat for lunch that
day, or whether I'd seen the previous night's episode of a TV show.
Those were all moments when I showed my students a glimpse
behind the Mrs. Watson curtain so they could see *me*: smaller, more
vulnerable, more real.

My best days of teaching were when I was *Angela Watson*. Mrs.
Watson ran the school day—she was always present, and always
focused on leading the students—but Angela was there, too. While

Mrs. Watson was teaching reading, Angela would make a snarky or sarcastic side comment about a character in the book and make all the kids laugh ("Yeah, good thinking, Hansel, stick your head in a witch's oven to see what's in there.") While Mrs. Watson was lining the kids up for recess, Angela would commiserate with the kids that she, too, had been waiting all morning to get out into the beautiful sunshine. While Mrs. Watson was helping students with a project, Angela would get the giggles over something random that wasn't even particularly funny and share it with the kids instead of suppressing it.

I don't think it's a stretch to say that the days when I was fully myself in the classroom were the best days for the kids, too.

Be a storyteller: draw inspiration for teaching curriculum from real-life events

One of the easiest ways to tap into students' natural curiosity about you and incorporate a more personable, relatable side of yourself is by sharing connections between your life and your curriculum. And since our brains are wired for storytelling, you'll discover that information sticks much better in kids' minds when it's in the form of a narrative.

Experiment with tying your curriculum to interesting anecdotes about things you experience outside the classroom:

When modeling how to respond to a writing prompt, use the movie you saw last weekend as your topic.

Ask the kids during science if they saw the latest museum exhibit and show the photos you took.

Talk about the incredible novel you're reading and how the author uses the best imagery or figurative language, or how you had to use context clues to figure out a word.

Play the National Geographic special you saw on TV and

recorded for the kids as part of your unit on world cultures.

Recount how you were having coffee with a friend and had a funny misunderstanding because of the homophones *pair* and *pear*.

Share with the kids how you used the term *parallel* when you were at a football game on Sunday.

Tell how you got in a playful disagreement with your spouse over the history of a neighborhood restaurant, and model how you used internet research skills to find out which one of you was right.

Retell the story of how you had to wait in an extremely long line at the store when you were late for a party, and share how you practiced using the de-stressing and problem solving strategies you'd taught your students.

Can you see all the possibilities here? Don't try to turn off your "teacher brain" when you leave the school building. Be on the perpetual lookout for new stories to tell your students and consider how you can use your daily life experiences to make instruction more relatable and meaningful. Allow yourself to draw inspiration from your outside interests, and take those experiences back to the classroom to enhance your lessons.

What does passionate, authentic teaching look like for YOU?

As you consider how to integrate your personal life with your teaching and incorporate your interests into your instruction, keep in mind that there's no set formula to follow. Passionate, authentic teaching is going to look different for each person.

Don't fight against your natural personality type. There's no need to try to be something you're not. Both introverted and extroverted teachers can be effective in the classroom. Passionate teachers can be silly or serious, outspoken or reflective: their passion just manifests differently based on who they are as people.

Maybe you're the kind of teacher who likes to jump up on tables to make a point and transform your classroom into a medieval castle before your students learn about the Middle Ages. By all means, go for it! But passionate teaching doesn't have to mean showy, loud, or dramatic. It can mean a dry sense of humor that causes the kids to hang onto your every word so they can catch the little sidebar jokes you make. It can mean a quiet inner strength. For me, it means a smile on my face and warmth in my voice.

It's perfectly fine if you're reading this and thinking to yourself, *I have no idea what passionate teaching looks like for me.* Here's how to figure it out.

Think back to a lesson that you really enjoyed teaching, one in which you were totally immersed in the content and fully present with your kids. Think of a lesson in which you looked up at the clock and were stunned to see only 10 minutes left in the class period, and you wondered, *Where did the time go?* Can you remember a lesson like that?

That's what passionate teaching looks like for *you.* That's the teaching persona you want to present to your kids on a daily basis. Chances are, that's your authentic self. Therefore, those are the kinds of lessons you want to teach all the time.

If you come alive in the classroom during lively experiments or skits, do more of them! If you love gathering students at your feet while you read a heart-tugging story, do that as often as you can. After all, no one is passionate about worksheets and practice tests. No teacher gets excited about making kids write their spelling words 5 times each. Though you may be required to implement some lessons you dislike, always look out for opportunities to integrate activities that you do enjoy.

If you only have one or two teaching strategies that you're super passionate about using, that's okay! Get really good at them, and add more over time. Variety is not the most important factor here— your enthusiasm is. If you are excited to teach the lesson, you are far more likely to get kids excited, too.

Beyond passionate teaching: be a passionate person

It's so important to let students into your life so they can relate to and bond with you, but that's only possible if you actually *have* a life to talk about. Someone who works all the time and has no outside interests is boring. And who wants a boring teacher?

The best teachers I know are genuinely interesting people. They have a unique and distinctive sense of humor. They actively look for fun opportunities to spend time with people they like. They have hobbies they are intensely passionate about—everyone in school knows they never miss a Yankees game, or drive past a craft store without stopping. They are voracious readers or are borderline obsessive about a particular TV series. Many of them are risk-takers, travelers, or extreme sport enthusiasts: they love activities that get their adrenaline pumping and take them out of their comfort zone.

You see, people who are passionate about teaching aren't just passionate about teaching. *They're passionate people, period.* They bring energy and enthusiasm to everything they do. They make the most of every moment in life. They're resilient and don't allow setbacks to steal their joy or dissuade them from accomplishing what they set out to do.

If you want to be a passionate teacher with unshakeable enthusiasm, you have to develop that trait in *your whole self*, not just the one compartment of your life that is devoted to work. You have to consciously make the choice to surround yourself with people and influences that inspire you to be a passionate person.

Your motivation at work is directly related to how you spend your personal time

I assure you from my own experience that passionate teaching is not rooted in lying around and complaining about work on

Facebook. If you don't do anything after school that is re-energizing, you're going to go back into the classroom the next day feeling even more depleted. The job will take even more out of you, and you're going to get sucked into a downward spiral.

I try to do something that is inspiring and energizing for me as a person on a daily basis. Even though I'm busy, this is the choice I consciously make because I know that the way I choose to spend my evenings makes a tremendous difference in my creativity level, attitude, and productivity the following day. I can't afford *not* to take care of myself, because everyone around me suffers if I don't.

For me, it's very important to get up early and have quiet time for prayer and meditation before all the demands of the day start coming at me. I also know I need to get fresh air: my mind just functions better if I take a walk, play tennis, spend time doing yardwork, or participate in some other outdoor activity, so I grab those opportunities whenever I can. A few evenings a week, I'll listen to inspiring podcasts while taking a walk, and then continue listening to them while I fix dinner and do the dishes instead of just having the TV blaring in the background while I cook.

After my husband and I eat and talk about our day, we spend some time relaxing together on the couch. I usually pull out my iPad to connect with friends online for a few minutes. I also browse Pinterest and Instagram to get some ideas for the classroom as well recipes and other resources I'm interested in. Before bed, I usually read a book for a few minutes. The book topics range from motivational to brain research to classic novels I enjoyed as a child and am now revisiting.

Spending time with people I love, taking care of myself, and pursuing my personal interests makes me feel more energized when I return to school. These activities feed my soul in a way that the "work 24/7 and then crash on the couch eating junk food" cycle never does.

No matter how tempting it is to fall into unhealthy habits after a long day of teaching and responsibilities at home, I have to *choose* to use my time in ways that nourish my body, mind, and soul. I have to purposefully surround myself with people and influences that are inspiring so that I can enter the classroom the next day and inspire my students.

Learn to manage your most important resource: energy

One day after a particularly tiring day at work, my husband called and asked me to pick up his clothes at the dry cleaner and put gas in the car.

I sighed. "Honey, I don't think I can get that done today."

"Really? It's only 4:00. I thought when you showed me your to-do list this morning, you had some time blocked out for running errands."

I paused. He was right, technically. I was leaving school and still had 7 hours left in the day before my usual 11 pm bedtime. Even though I needed to prepare dinner and take care of other tasks, I knew that picking up clothes at the dry cleaner and getting gas would take no more than 20 minutes out of my day. I had plenty of time.

What I didn't have was plenty of energy. *Physically*, I was too tired to run more errands.

The following day, we needed to sit down and go over some mortgage paperwork. It was not a particularly time-consuming task: maybe 10-15 minutes of filling out forms and making sure everything was accurate. It was also not a physically draining task, as I could complete it while sitting right on my couch.

And yet I put those forms off for nearly a week. I had the time, but I did not have the *mental* energy. My job required so much intense concentration that I didn't feel I was able to take on any other mentally demanding tasks after work.

Both of those incidents are pretty normal, and I don't think either one can be avoided altogether. There will sometimes be days when we feel mentally or physically drained of all energy after work, and that's okay. The point here is *awareness*. We must be aware of and plan to manage not only our time, but also our energy.

When you increase your energy level, you get more done

It's amazing how many hours can pass by unproductively when you don't have much energy. Every task takes twice as long because you're dragging your way through it. You allow yourself to get distracted and take far too many breaks. You procrastinate, pushing off your to-do list over and over again, hoping you will somehow have more energy in an hour than you do right now.

It's also amazing how much you can accomplish in just 10 or 15 minutes if you're highly energized. You can work at lightning speed and push through all obstacles without letting them faze you.

So, if you have an important task to do, which would you rather have, a lot of energy but just a little time? Or a lot of time but just a little energy?

I think the choice is obvious. Energy is one of our most important resources, but most of us give very little thought as to how we manage it and produce more of it. We don't consider ways to replenish both our physical energy levels and our mental energy levels.

Unlike that other precious resource, time, our energy level does not naturally replenish itself. Every morning that we are blessed to wake up, we are given more time. That is not true of energy. If you don't do anything the day before to re-energize yourself (including getting to bed at a decent hour), there's a good chance you will not wake up with more energy.

The secret to how some teachers "do it all"

You might be thinking at this point, *I have too much going on in my life. There's no way I could spend time every day on something that is relaxing or energizing for me.*

And yet, you can probably think of a few teachers who somehow manage to do it. I know an incredible seventh grade teacher who has four kids under age 7. She blogs and keeps up with social media, has written three books for teachers, travels for speaking engagements, and sets aside dedicated time for herself, her spouse, and each one of her children. She's in great physical shape and takes care of herself emotionally and spiritually.

She has the same amount of hours in the day that you and I have. Why do people like that get so much more done? Why are they able to bring passion and enthusiasm to everything they do while others are dragging through every little task?

The answer is simple: *they have more energy.* That makes them more efficient, and they're able to get more things accomplished in the same amount of time. Some of them are naturally fast workers, movers, and thinkers, and that helps tremendously. But people who seem to effortlessly accomplish a lot tend to do so mostly because they have more energy, and they have that energy for two main reasons.

Firstly, passionate and accomplished people make time for things that replenish their energy levels. They prioritize sleep, eating well, exercising, spending time with people they care about, and doing fun or restful things for themselves. They might not meet all those goals everyday, but they structure their lives so that the things that are important to them are given top priority.

Secondly, accomplished people tend to be extremely driven by a greater purpose. They have a clearly defined vision that motivates them to produce even when they're very tired. Their work in all areas of life is so meaningful to them that completing it actually gives them more energy rather than draining it away.

You can become that type of person! You can choose to make time for things that re-energize you physically and mentally. And, you can develop a sense of purpose that helps you persevere no matter what, in every task you do. That's what this book is all about. I'm going to share lots of ways you can integrate your authentic self into your teaching and make the things that energize you a priority so you can bring that passion to your classroom.

2

Allocate your time and energy wisely through productive routines

In the last chapter, we talked about the importance of having a rich personal life that informs and inspires your teaching, and how caring for yourself and spending time with people you love gives you more energy to teach. Now let's look at how to increase your productivity at school so you can have that needed time for your personal life.

The goal here is to get more done while expending less time and energy. We have to let go of the misperception that working longer hours means we're accomplishing more or that we're more dedicated to the profession. Staying at school until 6 pm every day does not automatically mean you're doing a better job teaching, and leaving at 3 pm doesn't necessarily mean you're less invested in your work.

Your *productivity level* is far more important than the number of hours you work. If you can learn to accomplish more in a shorter period, that leaves you with additional time to enjoy your family, hobbies, and downtime without shortchanging the people who depend on you at school. It's truly a win-win.

How many hours do you really *work* at school?

I'm sure you know of teachers who hang around the school building until dinnertime on a daily basis. Maybe you're even one of them! In most cases, those teachers are not doing schoolwork from 3-7 pm without stop. Part of their time is spent surfing the web, checking in on family members over the phone, and chatting with colleagues. While they're working, they're also eating snacks, watching afternoon talk shows, and responding to personal phone calls, emails, texts, and social media messages.

There's nothing wrong with doing any of those things when you're off the clock—but don't fool yourself into thinking you have no choice but to stay holed up in your classroom for four hours every day when the actual work portion of that time is more like three hours.

It's possible that you *think* you work 60-hour weeks but are only focused and productive for 40 or 50. If you can cut out the extraneous tasks that are distracting you from what's really important, you may find yourself with an hour or more of "free" time each day.

Be intentional with your time and go to school to WORK

I've talked with a number of educators who've managed to create lots of family time and keep teaching from taking over their lives. Each one of them has a different approach, but there's a common undercurrent to every one of their stories. They all follow the same basic principle: *Go to school each day with the mindset that you're there to work.*

You're not going to school to gossip with co-workers.

You're not going to school with a ten item personal to-do list that you want to squeeze in.

You're not going to school with the intention of checking

personal email and Facebook.

Think about how quickly those little diversions add up: one quick email reply leads to reading a short online article, which leads to checking the weather…and the next thing you know, thirty minutes have passed and the stack of papers on your desk hasn't been touched. Set your goals for the day, make your to-do lists, and get the work done.

Why early morning can be your most productive time

Given the choice between going to school early or staying late, I'd pick the former any time. In the afternoons, I'm far more likely to let exhaustion get the best of me, or get sucked into hanging out with my co-workers to chitchat.

Early mornings tend to be fairly quiet in most schools. All the staff who have arrived early are working feverishly in their classrooms and minding their own business. The day is still a blank slate: whatever happened yesterday is in the past, and the early morning is an opportunity to get organized and mentally prepared for the day ahead. Take advantage of that!

If you're not a morning person, you're probably resisting the idea of going to school early. I can completely relate. I used to sleep until the last possible moment and rush around like crazy to get ready for work. By the time I checked in to the office, spoke to colleagues in the hallway, and finally unlocked my classroom door, I had less than 15 minutes before the kids arrived.

I finally got the courage to move my alarm clock up an entire hour. What a difference that made in my attitude! I could have some quiet time on my apartment balcony and get my mind ready for the day ahead. (Bonus: the caffeine in my giant mug of coffee had time to kick in.) I arrived at school before parents were swarming the office and teachers were congregating in the hallways. I had a whole extra half hour to do whatever I needed to do in my classroom.

It was so much more pleasant to allow myself some margin rather than try to race out the door as quickly as possible each day. My stress level decreased significantly, since a train crossing during my morning commute or impromptu meeting with the guidance counselor no longer threw me hopelessly behind time. In turn, I noticed a big change in the level of patience and productivity I had during the day.

Two types of tasks you should never schedule for the morning

So how should you use your early morning time? That depends on your preferences, but I recommend that you don't start off your day by doing anything that puts you in a bad mood. This means when you leave school the day prior, you probably shouldn't delay in writing up a behavior referral, responding to that nasty email from a parent, or cleaning up the giant mess of supplies on your reading group table that one of your students "forgot" to take care of.

Know your own triggers: anything that gets your blood boiling should be done at the end of the day (if possible) so that when you leave the school building, you can let it go mentally and begin with a fresh start in the morning. Don't set yourself up to handle a bad situation first thing so that you're annoyed and irritable before the kids even enter the room.

The other thing you should never do in the morning is any task that's absolutely essential to the rest of your day. If you must have data organized for a lunchtime meeting or are relying on photocopies for your first period class, do *not* wait until 7 am to take care of it! You might get a flat tire and be late for school, a parent might show up for an unscheduled conference, or you may get drawn into a conversation with an administrator. Don't compound the problem of a schedule disruption by being stressed over an important task you put off until the last minute.

Create a pleasant morning ritual for an easy transition into your day

Use your time before the first bell to do things that get you excited about your day and make you feel prepared for your lessons. Double check to make sure your materials are organized and ready to go. Look through your lesson plans and get focused on your goals for student learning so you feel confident and focused on what really matters.

You might also want to create a morning ritual for yourself—a routine that you enjoy and that gets you in the mindset for teaching. I had a lot of colorful, decorative lamps in my classroom, and though I could have assigned a student the job of switching them all on, I enjoyed walking around my classroom in the morning with the overhead lights off, turning on one lamp at a time. I'd look at the space around the lamp and picture the learning that would take place there later in the day. Sometimes I'd pray over my classroom or just ask God to give me wisdom and fill me with love for my students.

I'd then turn on music that calmed me if I was anxious, or energized me if I was tired. I'd sit at my desk with a second cup of coffee and something simple for breakfast. As you know, a quiet moment to sit down at your desk in an empty classroom and listen to relaxing music with a cup of coffee is a huge luxury for a teacher, so this ritual was a very special way to begin the day.

As I sipped my coffee and ate, I went through my lesson plans for that day and made sure all the materials were organized and accessible. Many times, I'd alter the plans according to my mood, rearranging lessons a bit or incorporating a different activity that better suited my energy level, the weather, or a change in our daily schedule that was beyond my control. This was my last chance to deeply consider my students' needs and reflect on my practice before I'd have to think on my feet again.

When my plans were in place and my coffee was finished, I'd turn off the music and turn on the TV, which was tuned to the school's morning announcements channel. The school played kid-friendly, upbeat music on the channel until announcements started, so listening to that was the start of my transition into the hustle and bustle that would begin shortly. I'd do miscellaneous tasks around the classroom like handling email, intra-school mail, and paperwork.

When the first bell rang to indicate students would be coming down the hallways, I'd usually open my classroom door and stand in the entranceway. This was my chance to chat briefly with the teachers next door and across the hall, and then greet students as they entered the room. Before the kids even came into the classroom, I had a chance to connect with them, read their facial expressions and body language to get an idea of what kind of energy they were bringing to the classroom, and talk about anything they needed to discuss.

Teach warm up/bell work routines for whenever students enter the classroom

The arrival of students in the morning doesn't have to mean chaos begins. I spent a great deal of time in August teaching students how to enter the room quietly, take care of their own arrival tasks (pencil sharpening, getting a drink of water, and so on) and then begin their morning warm up activity. This freed me to remain by the doorway and continue greeting their classmates as each one arrived.

Having a warm-up routine also meant that I wasn't responsible for teaching from the moment the kids entered the room. Even when I taught PreK, my students learned to unpack and then sit on the rug and whisper-read books together. By teaching students to always follow the same morning routine, I was able to handle last-minute emergencies, bus incidents, tardies, and so on without throwing the rest of the class off schedule.

I used the same routine for after lunch and after special classes (like P.E. and music): students came into the room, looked at the board to read the warm up activity, and quietly got started. Usually the warm up would take between 5 and 20 minutes, depending on the type of task and also how much time I needed before the lesson began. If the secretary asked me to respond to an email immediately after lunch or students had gotten in a cafeteria argument and I needed to help problem solve, I could easily extend the warm up activity to buy myself a couple of extra minutes, and the students never knew the difference. I could wait to begin my instruction until I was completely ready and present in the moment.

I highly recommend that you create similar expectations in your classroom, and I'll explain how in chapter 14, Construct a Self-Running Classroom That Frees You to Teach. You'll need to model, practice, and reinforce your expectations for several weeks before the habit is ingrained in your students, but the payoff is worth it!

Never depend on your planning time break

I can't count the number of times I'd intended to get something done during my prep period and then gotten sidetracked by an "emergency" that left me unable to finish the task. I'd glance at the clock and realize that I was completely out of time, race over to pick up my students from art or P.E., and then frantically try to figure out an alternative lesson while the kids finished their warm-up. Lesson learned: planning time is not guaranteed, and if there's a task that must be done in order for me to teach a lesson after my planning time, I'd better handle it the day prior!

Over time, I realized that grading papers was one of the best tasks for me to do during my prep period. It was quiet, fairly interruptible, non-urgent, self-paced, and allowed me to listen to relaxing music while I worked. I'd select assignments that were quick and easy to grade so I could manage a stack of them in the short time I had available. Knowing that I'd only be able to grade for about 25 minutes helped keep me focused, and it was extremely rewarding to see the pile of papers diminished in such a short period of time.

I also liked using my prep time to do fairly mindless tasks like making copies, laminating, and straightening up the classroom. The key was to make sure that I was preparing materials several days ahead of time, so that it wouldn't be a problem if I couldn't finish. And if I did get it done, I'd actually be a day or two ahead on my lesson prep, making me feel even more accomplished.

De-stress during your prep period

There are certain days when it's a much better use of your planning time to get yourself back on firm emotional ground than to do anything teaching related. Sometimes you need your prep period to consist solely of sitting in a quiet, dark classroom while taking deep breaths and eating half a box of chocolates. (Only partly kidding about the chocolate.)

Can I encourage you to allow yourself that? You can always get work done on your lunch break, if need be. That pile of papers is not going anywhere, and chances are you will be a much better teacher when students return after your prep period if you just chill out for ten minutes than if you grade a handful of tests.

It's very important to decompress if you're in a bad mood during the school day, because if you don't, you'll take your bad mood out on the kids and be too exhausted to teach the way you need to.

Don't use the school day to tackle problems related to your personal life

Have you ever told yourself you'd just check your personal email for a second during your lunch break, only to find something upsetting waiting in your inbox that distracted you for the rest of the day?

I remember many occasions where I called my husband just to say hi and learned that our electric bill was double for the month, or the cat had gotten sick, or the car was making a weird ticking sound and needed to be taken to the shop.

Maybe you handle that stuff better than I do, but learning about personal problems in the middle of the teaching day completely zapped my ability to stay in the moment with my students, and it brought my energy level way down. Eventually I learned to wait and call my husband after school, or if I did call during the day, to tell him I needed to avoid talking about our household to-do list.

I've found that most minor problems can be put off for a few hours during the school day. For me, the job of teaching is just too demanding to try to attend to personal problems at the same time.

Choose a re-energizing or relaxing place to eat lunch

There are many veteran teachers who will advise you never to step foot in the teachers' lounge. They'll describe it as a place of complaining and whining, and tell you to avoid the lounge at all costs. Others will tell you it's essential to eat in the lounge so you can socialize with your co-workers, build relationships, and de-stress.

I don't have strong opinions on this. For me, it depended on the school and the group of teachers who shared my lunch shift. Some years, the lounge was a lot of fun, and other years, it was seriously depressing.

What worked for me during those years when I didn't enjoy the teachers' lounge was eating in a co-worker's room or having a co-worker join me for lunch in my room. Usually we'd turn the lights off: it's relaxing, and signals to anyone walking by that you're not around to answer "just one quick question." It was wonderful to eat with someone whose company I enjoyed without the chatter and background conversations that came with eating in the lounge. And since we were sitting in my classroom, I could usually get some work done for the last half of the break while we continued talking.

Other great options for utilizing your lunchtime

Some teachers find it easier to skip their lunch break in order to stay in high gear and power through the day. They find that if they allow themselves downtime instead of working through their break, they experience a drop in energy and end up staying later after school to make up for it.

Other teachers like to eat with their students in the cafeteria or invite kids to their classroom for lunch. This really goes a long way toward building rapport and getting to know your students as individuals. Of course, this means you don't get a break from kids or the chance to eat for five minutes without anyone asking you a question, so you could choose this option on a weekly or monthly basis if that works better for you.

Still other teachers swear by a solitary lunch period. They want to be left totally alone in their classrooms to have some time for themselves. I think that can be great, too. My advice is to experiment and see what works best for you, and be open to altering your routine as your circumstances and needs change.

After the kids leave: do mindless tasks first and stay in motion

I think almost every teacher secretly does a happy dance after the kids go home at the end of the day. Wait, that's not quite accurate. I think almost every teacher does a little happy dance *mentally* and then collapses at her desk chair and wonders how long it's going to be before she can get some rest. No matter how much you love teaching, it is very tiring work!

Right after the kids leave is a great time to do tasks that don't require much mental energy, like erasing the board, straightening desks, and organizing materials. Tackle anything that's not going to require much of your depleted mental reserves, especially since focusing will probably be made harder by loudspeaker announcements and co-workers stopping by.

I've found that sitting "just for a minute" makes it even harder to get up and do other tasks around the room afterward. For me, it's better to stay in motion after getting the kids out the door, and save all the seated tasks (like paperwork and computer-based stuff) for last.

Check your school email only when everything else is done

Sitting down right after school to get on the computer not only makes it harder for me to get back up and do other tasks, but it also leaves me vulnerable to the powerful time suck that is the internet. It's almost impossible for me check school email right after dismissal and then close the laptop and do something tedious like grade papers. I end up checking personal email, reading breaking news stories, connecting with friends on social media…and then nothing else gets done.

But, if I wait to check school email until right before I'm ready to go home, I can respond to parents' and administrators' messages with a single-minded focus because I know that the moment I'm done, I can leave. When I get a message that requires a lengthy response or some sort of action on my part, I either take care of it quickly or return to it once I'm home and have had a chance to relax first. Personally, I'd rather return email messages at home in the evenings than leave my classroom a mess because the only thing I was able to do after school was respond to an email. I refuse to let last minute email requests throw off the important work I had planned.

If your principal requires you to check email throughout the day, consider having push notifications sent to your phone so you can quickly glance at your phone screen to see if there are any urgent emails without having to unlock your phone or open your computer. Be sure to turn your personal notifications off during the day, and turn the work notifications off in the evening!

Alternatively, choose two specific times during the school day to look at work email, such as 10 minutes before school starts and 10 minutes before your planning period ends. That should be ample time to read and respond to anything that's urgent and you'll have no choice but to logout after a few minutes because students will start arriving.

Take it home or stay late?

Once your quick, easy, and most urgent tasks are done in the afternoons, you can decide whether you want to delve into more taxing projects or take them home. There's no point in working long hours if you're not really working, so you have to know your own habits here. If you're overly tired, someone is constantly coming in and asking you for things, or you're tempted to wander next door to chat, pick your overtime hours wisely...or complete them at home.

Some days I wanted to just knock out all my work so I could leave and forget about school for awhile. Other times I looked around at all the stuff that needed to be done in my messy classroom and pictured myself sitting on my comfortable couch with a mug of hot tea next to my papers, and I raced out the door in a split second with a bag of stuff trailing behind me. Giving myself the choice of where to do the work made it a little less painful to complete.

The 40 Hour Teacher Workweek

If you want to learn more tips about productivity and time management, visit 40HTW.com. That stands for the 40 Hour Teacher Workweek, and it's a set of resources (including free videos) I've created to help you design a workable daily schedule and shave 10+ hours from your grading, lesson planning, and more. Even more importantly, the 40HTW will help you align your lifestyle with your values so you're able to make time for the things that matter most. I promise it will be transformative for you *and* your family.

I'm going to delve into more of the 40HTW topics in the next two chapters, because I think they're an essential part of getting full enjoyment from teaching. Let's look at establishing boundaries around your time, and figuring out how to prioritize what matters most in your job and in your life.

3

Establish healthy habits for bringing work home and decompressing

Letting go of the workday each evening is one of the biggest problems I hear from teachers who feel like they don't have time to do everything that's important in their lives. Many of them have established cut-off times for working at home, but haven't been able to find a way to stop *thinking* about work when they're with their families.

Brainstorming, daydreaming, and planning are all healthy, productive habits. But there's a difference between planning and worrying, and a difference between preparing for the future and rehashing the past. There's also a big difference between thinking about a lesson at 7 pm and worrying about an evaluation at 2 am.

I don't think there's a teacher alive who hasn't grappled with these issues, or woken up in the middle of the night full of concern about a student. So, how do you get schoolwork done at home without letting it consume your life? How do you turn off those anxious thoughts when it's time to rest? Let's look at some strategies for creating healthier, more productive habits.

Decompress with ONE co-worker

After students went home in the afternoon, I often found it helpful to stop by the classroom of a close friend at school. If it had been a really tough day, I'd swing by her room immediately after dismissal so I could get things off my chest and go back to my room to work. On a more typical day, I'd stop by on my way out of the building. 5-15 minutes of conversing about how our lessons went, how our kids behaved, and so on was usually enough to help me leave the day's issues behind when I got in my car and went home.

So why only one co-worker? Firstly, the whole school doesn't need to know your business. Most of your co-workers will never see you teach and will judge you based on the way you present yourself. Telling anyone who will listen that you can't handle your students and feel hopelessly overwhelmed by your work doesn't do much for your professional reputation.

The other reason to confide in only one co-worker is that it's rare that anything productive will result from complaining about the same situation multiple times. The more you talk about your problems, the more you allow those problems to take up space in your head. The things that you think and talk about create emotions, and if you're repeatedly going over all the bad things that happened in your day, you're going to find yourself feeling burned out and depressed.

The person you choose as your confidante should be someone you respect as a teacher. If she or he is only going to offer you unprofessional advice or make you feel like your situation is impossible, what's the point in talking about it?

Your confidante should also be someone who respects you in return. There's nothing worse than confiding in someone and feeling like they're judging you or planning to gossip about your failures to other people in the school. Your confidante should be someone who listens carefully and offers you helpful advice, and you should do the same for him or her.

It can take a while to find that one person you can safely and productively decompress with. This kind of relationship can't be rushed, so be prepared to go slowly and be very mindful of the tone of your conversations with others. It's better to have no one to confide in at school than to pour your heart out to someone negative or untrustworthy.

Take time to socialize and celebrate with colleagues

Though I don't think it's healthy to vent to a large group of your co-workers or teacher friends, I do think it's a great idea to spend time with them socially. No one understands what it's like to be a teacher except other teachers. Spending time with co-workers after school can allow you to feel less isolated and alone in your stress, and therefore more equipped to let those stresses go once you're home.

I taught for several years in a school in downtown Fort Lauderdale, Florida, where a wonderful teacher named Linda occasionally invited the entire staff over to her home. She lived in a cute little cottage with a small tropical oasis out back: a pool, hot tub, tiki bar, and comfortable lounge chairs. I still treasure those days of sitting around in her backyard under the palm trees, just enjoying the company of my co-workers.

There are few of us who are able to offer that kind of relaxing environment to our guests, but we can all get the ball rolling by inviting our grade level team or other teacher friends to simple, laid-back social events. I always lived in small apartments and couldn't fit more than a handful of people in my living room at a time, but I was well-known in my schools as the "social director" who would reach out to teacher friends to put together a happy hour event at a local restaurant. Though the 2 for 1 drink specials were a special treat for some people, alcohol was not the center of the occasion and often no one drank. What we really depended on was time to sit, relax, talk, and enjoy some good food together.

Some years, our happy hour was a weekly tradition; other years, monthly or even quarterly. There were times when husbands came along because they wouldn't have had much time with their wives in the evenings otherwise. There were also times when kids came along because some teachers had no one to watch their little ones. For our close-knit group, that was fine! The important thing was that we were able to spend time together.

I've noticed that the tougher the working environment, the more likely teachers are to create social activities with one another. I know many inner city teachers who cling to an afternoon happy hour like it's life support—not because of the drinking, necessarily, but because of the bond they have with their colleagues. When you deal with outrageously stressful issues all throughout the week, there's no one else who is going to understand what you experienced besides your co-workers, and finding time to spend with them is critical.

Make the most of your commute home

The time spent traveling after school can be instrumental in helping you decompress so you don't bring work problems home. I like to use my time in the car or on the subway to think through anything that didn't work that day and create a plan for the next day.

If something negative that happened is bothering me when I leave school, I allow myself to think about it for a few minutes and then create some kind of mental reframing that allows me to stop worrying about it. (I'll share more about that process at the end of this chapter.) So, even if I still have schoolwork to do in the evening, at least I can relax in knowing that I won't need to mentally replay a confrontation with a student or rehearse what I'll say in a parent conference the next day. My mental work of processing the day's events is done.

I always find it helpful to listen to positive and encouraging music during my commute. You know that one song that instantly puts a smile on your face every time you hear it? Listen to that right after school. In fact, you can put together an entire playlist of songs that are uplifting to you, and after you've mentally processed your day, lose yourself in the song lyrics and your favorite beats.

If you don't have any alone time on your commute because you carpool or drive your children home, consider taking 5 minutes for yourself in your classroom before you leave for the day. Put on a song that is relaxing or peaceful, and give yourself just a couple minutes of downtime to process and mentally celebrate what you've accomplished in the past few hours. Then, embrace your shared commute—talking to others can be a great distraction from your own day and can help put your problems into perspective.

Create flexible and realistic expectations for how much work you can do at home

I don't like to make a decision in advance about how much work I'm going to do in the evenings because things rarely go the way I plan. I find that unexpected events usually pop up at the last minute, causing me to feel stressed out because I wasn't able to get my work done. I then end up dragging a full bag of completely untouched work right back into the classroom the following day.

So, I try to be flexible about how much I'm planning to get done in the evenings and not create unrealistic expectations for myself. On the weekends, I usually make Saturdays my work-free day so I can get errands done, have some fun, and generally put distance between myself and whatever I'm dealing with at work.

Since I'll inevitably be thinking about school again by Sunday evening, it makes more sense to me to get work done then. Waiting until Sunday morning to decide how much work I'll do allows me to roll with the punches if I'm not feeling well or if an opportunity to do something fun comes up.

Aim for small blocks of highly focused work time

Teaching is a never-ending job and there will always be something more that you could do, so there's no point in trying to work until it's all finished. Unless you have a special deadline (like report cards are due), try to choose how much of your free time you're willing to dedicate to your work.

Can you steal two hours while your little one naps? Can you squeeze in an hour before the family wakes up and another after they go to bed? Figure out what will make a dent in your workload in order to make the next day go more smoothly, and do only that amount.

Grabbing just an hour or two here and there can actually be very productive if you make your work time a true work-only period. Remember when we talked about focusing only on school stuff during the workday? The same thing applies to your work time at home. If you choose to dedicate the hours of 7-9 pm to grading papers, do it wholeheartedly. Don't keeping checking your social media accounts. Don't watch TV. And definitely don't sit in the middle of the family room where other members of your household are going to interrupt you every five minutes!

Spending your time halfway in work mode and halfway in home mode will only prolong the amount of time you *perceive* yourself as working. Before you know it, the whole day will be gone and you'll be moaning about how all you did was work when the truth is that you only truly worked for an hour or two.

Tell your family you'd rather spend two hours holed up in your bedroom working single-mindedly and have the rest of the day to enjoy together than to spend four hours halfway present with them in front of the TV. Use that limited amount of quiet, isolated work time to motivate you toward maximizing every moment. And when the time is up, that's it—go back to your family and home priorities.

When you force yourself to stick to the time you allotted, staying focused gets much easier. If you're really going to put away the work at 5 pm, you don't have time to stop and peruse Instagram for a little break…and you know that you *can* go on Instagram guilt-free afterward because your work time is done.

Create a schedule each week for the time you'll work outside of contractual hours

I shared in the first chapter that I think it's good to spend some of your time in the evenings and on weekends doing things that inspire you professionally. I often spend my free time looking online for new lesson ideas or creating teaching resources while I watch TV because those are tasks I really enjoy. They don't feel like work, I'm under no obligation to complete them, and I don't choose to do them every single evening. I can easily spend a few hours in the evening creating and discovering new teaching materials, and I generally don't limit that time.

But my "work-work", the stuff I really don't want to do at home but can't possibly fit into my contractual hours at school? *That* I definitely place a limit on.

Some teachers find it helpful to dedicate set work hours for themselves. For example, they are committed to leaving school every day by 5 pm, no matter what, and they don't bring anything home.

Or, they leave more or less on time, but set aside the hours of 9:00-10:30 pm to do schoolwork almost every night. Others like to stay late or come in extra early on set days of the week, and don't do any overtime on the other days.

Many times, I preferred to leave school at 3 pm on Friday and get my weekend started, then take a few hours on Sunday afternoon to prep for the following week. I know another teacher who stays at school until 5 pm on Fridays and then does a few more hours of work that evening so she can completely relax on Saturday and Sunday. Other teachers prefer to do a little bit of work early on Saturday and Sunday mornings before their kids wake up.

Regardless of the structure you choose, I do encourage you to set boundaries around how many hours you will spend entering grades into your computer and completing other less-than-enjoyable tasks. Schoolwork tends to expand and take up however much time you allot, up to and including your entire evening or weekend. You have to make a conscious decision about how much prominence those tasks will play in your life.

Try to create loose guidelines and revise them as often as needed. You're probably going to need to work long hours at the start of the school year, so plan for a demanding schedule during back-to-school time and gradually ease up.

Your schedule can even vary from week to week. Sit down on Sunday evenings or Monday morning with your personal or family calendar and decide where schoolwork fits into your life for the week ahead. Maybe you'll decide to go into school an hour early each day and spend some time on Sunday afternoon grading papers. Next week, you might decide to go in 90 minutes early on Thursday and Friday and then do nothing school-related all weekend so you can enjoy relatives who are visiting.

Whatever you choose, have an end goal in mind. Decide *before* the week starts what your game plan will be so when Friday comes, you don't end up completely overwhelmed by all the things you didn't accomplish.

2 types of tasks you might want to do at home

The goal is to spend your evenings and weekends doing the things you enjoy most, so try to bring home the work you get personal satisfaction from completing.

I prefer to complete my "work-work" tasks during the course of an 8 hour day (grading, paperwork, photocopies, etc.) and then do the more creative tasks at home (designing projects for students, planning activities, and so on.) It's not always possible, but it's a helpful guideline I've set for myself.

You might also want to take home the tasks that you complete more effectively and efficiently when you're not in your classroom. For example, I would rather grade essays and lengthy assignments at home because it's more comfortable than sitting at my desk at school for two hours.

I also do my best lesson planning at home. I like to plan entire units at a time, so I need several hours to reflect deeply and get everything in order. I actually look forward to spending one weekend a month planning out all the cool activities I'm going to be doing with students—it gets me excited to go back to school on Monday morning.

Develop the right mindset for doing work at home

I hate washing dishes. In New York City, very few apartments have dishwashers or garbage disposals, and I always resented the amount of time I spent scrubbing pots and cleaning gunk out of the drain. I'd stand at the sink and fume, wondering for the millionth time why on earth our rent was so high and I still didn't have a machine to do my dishes.

One day I was in a particularly good mood and was singing a song to myself. I was thinking about how delicious and healthy the meal was, and enjoying the feel of warm water on my hands as I reflected on all the ways the evening had been a good one. Before I knew it, the dishes were done.

I wish I could tell you I'm now able to replicate that experience every time I have to do dishes. I'm not. And I still don't enjoy dishwashing. But when I take the time to put myself in the right mindset, it's a lot less unpleasant.

The same is true with doing schoolwork at home. You cannot allow yourself to continually think thoughts such as, *I shouldn't have to bring work home. This is so unfair. This job is killing me! I can't do this anymore. I deserve to have my evenings and weekends free.*

It doesn't matter if some of those thoughts are true—they're not healthy. They make working more miserable than it has to be and cause you to hate your job.

Create an enjoyable routine for working at home

The ideal way for me to grade papers is sitting in my pajamas in a comfortable chair with pleasant lighting. I like to have a blanket on my lap, the cat lying beside me, and a cup of tea on the table. Most of the time, I also want my favorite music turned on—I have a playlist of instrumental music that's perfect for relaxing background noise while working.

When I set up conditions like that, I'm much less resentful about doing work at home. I tell myself, *At least I'm not sitting in the classroom right now—I'm in my favorite chair, snuggled up with my cat. Not a bad way to spend an evening.*

If you're really consistent with this, you can create an almost Pavlovian response in yourself so that as soon as the routine is set, your mindset is automatically focused on schoolwork. Each time you sit in a certain chair listening to a certain album, your mind will gear up for the task at hand.

Motivate yourself to complete tasks by seeking out purpose

If you choose to focus on the end goal of the work you do in your free time, it will become a lot more pleasant. So, instead of thinking, *Alright, let me grade this stupid stack of papers*, choose a statement like one of these to repeat to yourself:

Grading these papers is going to tell me how well my students learned what I taught them this week.

I'm going to look for at least three students' papers that prove the work I did in class mattered.

I'm going to see how many students' names I get to cross off this standards checklist because they've mastered the content.

When I'm finished grading these papers, I'll know so much more about my students' needs and I'll be even more prepared for tomorrow.

Don't focus on all the laminating you have to cut out. Tell yourself, *When I'm done cutting, I'm going to have a brand new set of centers. My students are going to love them!*

Don't focus on all the data you have to record. Tell yourself, *When I'm done typing this, I'll have a clear record to show exactly what each student has mastered.*

Sure, some of these statements might be overly optimistic. But what would you rather do, grade essays or see how well your students learned to write an introductory paragraph? Frame the task so that it gives you a meaningful payoff, whatever that might be.

Spend at least 5 minutes each night preparing for the morning

I'm not very good with following my own advice here, but I sure like waking up knowing that I've already filled the coffee pot, picked out my outfit for the day, packed my lunch, and gathered all the things I need to bring to school.

These are little tasks, which, if left undone, tend to make me feel rushed in the morning and cause me to be late for work. Knowing that they're already taken care of makes for a much more peaceful night's sleep and gives me more margin in my routine the next day.

Of course, when I'm tired in the evenings, the last thing I feel like doing is packing my lunch. So I often promise myself that I only have to spend 5 minutes at night getting ready for the morning. Most of the time, I get on a roll and keep going until everything's done, but if I don't, at least that's 5 minutes less work I'll have to face when the alarm goes off in the morning.

Set a time frame for thinking about school in the evenings and on weekends

It's very stressful to have your mind constantly wandering into the future, running through the list of things you still need to get done and worrying about what the following day will hold.

You can limit this by giving yourself 5-15 minutes to *think* about school (apart from any actual work time you've dedicated.) I like to have a short time for thinking before I do schoolwork in the evening to get the big picture of what I need to accomplish, and then a few minutes again after I finish the work to give myself some closure.

If you're not bringing any work home for the evening but still find your mind wandering to your to-do list, try giving yourself 5-15 minutes to think about work. Set a timer if you need to. Or, think everything over while in the shower or vacuuming, and change your thought process when the activity is done.

Use your 5-15 minutes to plan out strategies for dealing with challenging issues. Write down any additional tasks you need to complete. Daydream about activities you want to do with your students. Envision yourself having a successful week. Then, shut down the anxious, problem-solving part of your brain for the evening and relax.

Train yourself not to worry about school outside of the time you allotted

In my book *Awakened: Change Your Mindset to Transform Your Teaching*, I share four mental strategies for dealing with unwanted thoughts: dismiss, distract, reject, and replace. Use those strategies when you're supposed to be relaxing but your mind keeps returning to all the pressures of teaching.

Tell yourself, *I am rejecting these thoughts about school because they're not productive. I'm choosing to replace them with the thought that when Monday morning comes, I can trust myself to know what to do, so I don't need to think about it right now.* Then distract yourself by doing something more enjoyable, and dismiss any thoughts about school that continue to arise.

It takes a while to discipline your mind to stay in the present moment, but each time you do it, you're breaking those unhealthy habits and making it easier to be mindful next time.

Choose strong replacement thoughts for issues that worry you

I found that one of the hardest aspects of teaching in high-poverty communities was not allowing my students' home lives to interfere with my own. As a new teacher, I often cried on the way home from school and again at night when I should have been sleeping because I was so worried about my students.

A particularly tough time of day for me was dinner. I'd sit down to the table and feel an overwhelming sense of sadness, knowing that many of my kids did not have a meal to eat. My family got very tired of seeing me so forlorn at meal times and I realized it was really unfair to allow myself to be depressed over my students.

Eventually, I had to choose a little inner monologue to repeat to myself before meal times:

I can't control what's happening in students' homes, and upsetting myself about it only ruins my own meal—it doesn't make things better for the kids. I have alerted the guidance counselor and made sure the family service worker is checking in on the kids regularly. That's my responsibility, and I did it. In this moment, the only thing I need to do is be present with my own family and enjoy the meal we're sharing. That way I won't be worn down and emotionally drained tomorrow when I'm with my students again.

The moment I started feeling sad or anxious, I'd repeat that set of replacement thoughts to myself, multiple times if needed. I'd then distract myself by focusing on the present moment, the delicious meal we were eating, and the people I was sharing it with.

I highly recommend that you identify the incidents that trigger anxiety for you about work and write out a set of replacement thoughts. You can then read and repeat them to yourself whenever needed.

For example, if you often wake up feeling dread or anxiety about the workday ahead, tell yourself,

If I'm feeling a sense of dread, then I must have been thinking some negative thoughts about work. I don't have to pay attention to those thoughts or feelings! Today I'm going to act rather than react, have flexible

expectations, and practice keeping a positive attitude. I'm setting my intent: I accept whatever comes my way and trust that I can handle it. Any challenges are just a chance to practice healthy mental and emotional habits. I'm looking forward to the opportunity to make a difference with my students. Every day is different, and I'm excited to see what things I can teach and learn today.

If you physically left school an hour ago, but your mind is still on your incomplete to-do list, tell yourself,

I accept the fact that I've done everything I can do today. Rather than focus on all the things that I left undone, I'm going to make a mental list of everything I accomplished: I talked to my assistant principal and everything will be handled with that student's behavior referral. I got my grades entered into the computer. I made a wonderful connection with my new student during reading instruction. I helped Mr. Lamont troubleshoot his printer; we finally got started on the solar system project...oh, and I figured out how to help Marcus understand the difference between adjectives and adverbs! This was actually a very productive day! Let me see what other good things I can recall...

If you can't sleep because you're worried about a parent conference in the morning, tell yourself,

I don't feel like going to bed now, but I'm going to choose not to live by my feelings. The wisest course of action is to get a good night's rest so I'll be fresh in the morning. I don't know how the conference is going to go, but I trust that I'll say and do the right thing when the time comes. I've written down my key points so I can let it go for right now. The only thing I need to do is relax, rest, and eat a healthy breakfast in the morning. I have faith that my inner wisdom will surface when I need it. Whatever happens tomorrow, I know I'll be able to handle it!

Recognize the difference between being unproductive and wasting time

I used to think that if I didn't collapse into bed at the end of the day completely exhausted, that meant I had not pushed myself to work to my full potential. If I had the energy to do just one more thing, I felt obligated to do it. I did not feel a sense of accomplishment unless I'd expended every last drop of energy I had to give.

One day as I was listening to a time management podcast, I realized how unbalanced my approach had become. When and how did exhaustion become the standard for a productive day? Why wasn't I satisfied with knowing that I got my important tasks done?

I decided to try scheduling downtime into my calendar: 8-9 pm was now going to be set aside for watching my favorite shows with my husband on our DVR. I realized that having a scheduled downtime freed me from the guilt of doing "nothing" and feeling like I should be tackling my to-do list, since watching the show together was one of the tasks I'd written down and intended to complete that day!

This system also motivated me to work more quickly and efficiently. I knew I needed to stop whatever else I was doing right at 8 pm, so I didn't have time to waste. I worked with intention, and then I relaxed with intention.

It turns out there's a big difference between wasting time and being unproductive. When I intended to get work done but ended up watching TV to avoid the task, I felt annoyed with myself. That was wasting time. But when I put everything else to the side and allowed myself to be present in a moment of relaxation with my family, it felt really, really good. I realized that I *was* being productive. I was accomplishing something that was important to me: bonding with people I care about and taking time to enjoy life.

Create alignment between your priorities and how you spend your time

Obviously your contractual hours at school are non-negotiable, and they're an important priority because they allow you to pay your bills. But when you let schoolwork dictate the rest of your life's schedule and try to squeeze in periods of fun and relaxation whenever you can, you're not going to end up with much time to regroup. So, do the reverse: block out periods of time in your day's schedule for top priorities, and pencil in the rest of your work and personal tasks around them.

If you truly believe that your family comes first, schedule them in first. If you tell yourself that being healthy is the most important thing, schedule in time for exercise, sleep, and healthy meals first. Your schoolwork beyond contractual hours can only be allowed to fill in the *leftover* times on evenings and weekends.

You probably won't be able to spend as much time as you'd like on the things that are really important to you, and that's okay. The key is to make sure that the way you spend your time is aligned with what you say you value most. Create time for the people and activities you care about most *before* you make time for work. Block off periods of time that are sacred and cannot be infringed upon by the pile of papers in your work bag.

By dedicating specific periods of time to what's most important in life, you are giving yourself permission to truly enjoy those things rather than feel mentally pulled in ten different directions. Be intentional: set aside time for your spiritual life, time for your family, time for your health, time for work, and so on...then stick to it.

Your schedule might look different every day, and there will be times when one aspect of life demands more attention than the others. That's fine. Just stay mindful of this on a daily basis, being vigilant about finding blocks of time you can dedicate to your biggest priorities in life.

Block off periods of time for "mental vacations"

You might even want to schedule a few longer blocks of time for mental vacations. Look at your calendar at the beginning of each week or month and figure out what's feasible. It might be an hour one evening, or an entire Saturday each month, depending on your other obligations. Write your mental vacation on your calendar and schedule it into your to-do list so that nothing else can interfere.

Use the time you set aside for a mental vacation to do something you'd do if you were on a physical vacation: take a nap, read a book, relax in a bubble bath, watch movies, eat an indulgent meal, or participate in an activity you enjoy but rarely get to experience due to time or monetary constraints. If you need a vacation with your family or friends, include them in the activity, blocking off work-free hours to enjoy spending quality time together.

During these times of scheduled relaxation and mental vacations, practice being truly present in the moment and enjoying time for yourself. You'll then be able to return to your work with more energy and focus later on.

4

Determine how to do what matters most and let go of the rest

Part of the reason why teaching can be so overwhelming and stressful is because there's always something more that you could be doing. There are also constant demands rushing at you from every side, and it can be challenging to figure out which ones deserve your time and energy and how to schedule them all in.

I have observed a lot of teachers over the years, and I can say without a doubt that one major difference between an effective, accomplished, confident teacher and one who is running around like a headless chicken is the ability to prioritize.

Let me give a hypothetical example.

Mr. Jackson sits down at his desk during his lunch break with the intention to quickly sort through the pile of papers that were in his intra-school mailbox and then start planning his lesson for the afternoon.

The phone rings almost as soon as he sits down. He stops to answer the call, which is a request from a colleague to share a teaching resource she asked for previously. He puts down his mail, spends five minutes hunting for the book his colleague needs, and then walks downstairs to bring it to her.

When he enters her classroom, he sees that another colleague is there, telling a story about an irate parent. Mr. Jackson hangs around to listen and commiserate.

He finally goes back to his classroom ten minutes later and a student is standing outside his door, saying she needs to leave early and came back to the room to get her things and copy the homework assignments.

Mr. Jackson doesn't have the homework ready yet, so he walks the student down to the office to make the photocopies. While there, the principal reminds him that his RTI documentation is due the following afternoon, so when Mr. Jackson gets back to the classroom, he stares at his desk, wondering if he should start entering the data into the computer now or do it later.

Suddenly, the after-lunch bell rings. Mr. Jackson realizes he hasn't eaten or regrouped. He also hasn't been very productive. He scrambles to get his lesson materials together, tossing the mail onto a large stack of papers and searching around for his teacher's guide.

The students are racing around the room, wound up from lunch and recess, and before Mr. Jackson can get them settled, a child asks for help unzipping a stuck jacket. Mr. Jackson struggles with the zipper for several minutes while the class gets crazier and out of control.

At that very moment (of course!), the principal walks in for a surprise observation. Mr. Jackson is hungry, tired, overwhelmed, and completely unprepared for the afternoon. He's been on his feet working nonstop and yet nothing important got accomplished. He can't even remember what he spent the last hour doing.

Mr. Jackson will try to start fresh tomorrow, but will quickly get sidetracked by last minute requests and interruptions all over again. The pattern will continue day after day after day, until he starts to wonder, *Why am I in this field? I don't think I'm cut out to be a teacher.*

This job is just too much work. I'm constantly falling further behind and just can't catch up, no matter what I do.

If you recognize yourself in Mr Jackson, I have good news for you: there is a better way. I'm going to teach you to figure out how to do what's really important and forget the rest.

You can't do it all and everything is not equally important

When your job starts to feel completely overwhelming, chances are good that you've either lost sight of your priorities or never set them to begin with. You've allowed so many tasks to pile up on your plate that they all seem equally important, and it feels like the world will come crashing down if you don't complete them all. Right now. Perfectly.

If you're not sure whether a task is important, ask yourself, *What would happen if I didn't do this?* For example, what would the consequence be for not rewriting every misspelled word on every student's paper? How would your lesson go if the worksheet you create doesn't have adorable clip art? What would be the result of not color-coding your filing system, creating a lengthy welcome packet for your student teacher, or changing your bulletin board borders on a monthly basis?

You can do anything, but you can't do everything. You must determine which tasks are really critical by asking yourself, *What will happen if don't do this?* If you can live with the result of not completing a task, write it in the low priority section of your long term to-do list so you can get to it later...or remove it altogether.

Urgent and important aren't always the same

Nearly all issues that crop up during the school day seem earth-shattering at first glance. But everything that feels like an emergency is not an emergency. Ask yourself, *What will happen if I do this later? Can this be handled in a few minutes? A few hours? A few days?* Do not let other people's last minute requests drive your schedule. That doesn't mean you ignore the work and let them down, it just means you choose a more convenient time to accommodate them.

When your team leader announces she needs a set of forms completed by the end of the school day, don't stop your grading immediately to fill them out. Write "Finish forms" on the day's to-do list and stay focused on the task at hand.

When a parent tries to corner you in the parking lot to talk about family drama, say, "I need to finish planning this science activity your daughter's going to do tomorrow morning—it's going to be incredible, I know she'll tell you all about it! Can I schedule a conference with you Thursday afternoon when I'm free and can really focus on what you're telling me?"

When a student asks you to write a recommendation letter or something else outside the scope of your usual instructional tasks, tell him, "Sure! As I explained in my policies at the beginning of the year, I don't have time during the school day to work on that, but I give up one of my Saturdays each month to help out. I can have the letter to you in two weeks."

You are in control of how you manage your time. Ultimately, you are responsible for your time management and productivity. If a last-minute or urgent request is not critical, you can choose when to complete it.

Figure out the most important task of the day and do it first

When planning out your tasks for the day, ask yourself, *What is the one thing I can do today that will allow me to leave work feeling a real sense of accomplishment?* There are many things you need to get done, but chances are, there's *one thing* that's more important than everything else.

Maybe you have a pile of two week-old tests you feel guilty about not having graded yet and it weighs on you every time you look at them.

Maybe you're being observed the next day and haven't even begun to think about what lesson you'll teach.

Maybe you have an IEP meeting and are feeling anxious because your documentation isn't in order.

These urgent, important tasks will create anxiety if you procrastinate and focus on other work. So write down your one thing—the most important task of the day, the task you cannot feel happy leaving undone when you drive out of the school parking lot that afternoon. If it's too hard to choose which task is most important, pick the hardest one (the task that you most dread and are likely to keep putting off.) *Then get that task done first.*

If you have to wake up early in order to make time for it, do that! You will feel a tremendous sense of accomplishment when you get the hardest or most important task taken care of right away, and that feeling of productivity will set the tone for your entire day.

Write down ALL your tasks and plug them into a schedule

Do you ever think of something that needs to be done and tell yourself, "Eh, I don't need to write this down. I'll remember." Don't do that to yourself! You need to write *everything* down.

If you don't write a task down, you have to use your very limited short term memory to hold that task in your brain. Having too many tasks circling around your mind feels stressful and causes your focus to suffer.

Every time you try to attend to something else important that day or go to sleep that night, your brain will be screaming, *Don't forget!* This creates tremendous anxiety and mental overwhelm. So whenever you think of something that needs to be done, *write it down immediately* so you can clear space in your mind for other things.

I do not recommend writing tasks on a four page (and growing) to-do list where they'll get buried and appear impossible to complete. It's very hard for most of us to tackle a list with more than a handful of things on it.

The system I suggest involves writing down all the tasks that need to get done in a prioritized list for the month, and then scheduling them into your day. You can do this with online tools and apps, or a paper version. I'll explain the paper version here, but you can easily replicate the same thing using a digital system that syncs across all your devices.

If you choose to use the paper version, you should also have some kind of tool that makes it easy to record tasks whenever you think of them. Sometimes we remember things when we're driving or getting ready for bed, and if you can quickly enter them on your phone, it will take very little time to add them to your to-do list the next day at school.

I have a two page prioritized to-do list you can download from unshakeablebook.com for free. The second page has space for a list of tasks to do at school and at home, divided into three sections (high, medium, and low priority.) The first page has daily to-do lists. When you think of a random task that needs to be done, write it on the second page under the appropriate priority level. Then when you plan out today's list of things to do, write in anything urgent or last minute, and choose a few things from your high priority list on the second page.

On days when you have a lot of tasks (or some very intensive ones), write in just the last-minute stuff and maybe one high priority item on the day's to-do list. On slower days or when you have lots of short tasks to do, you can add in some things from your medium and low priority lists, too.

If you find it difficult to manage and prioritize even short daily to-do lists, try creating a daily list which is divided into sections: *before school, planning time, lunch break, after school,* and *at home.* In the morning (or the night before), choose tasks from the prioritized to-do list and plug them into the schedule so you know exactly what to do when.

Be realistic! It's better to plan too few tasks and have extra time for choosing more from your long-term, prioritized list than to over-plan and feel discouraged because you're behind. You may even want to leave one of those time periods open for handling emergencies and catching up.

The goal during your workday should be to finish as much of your planned work as possible. The majority of our tasks as teachers tend to be unplanned, but that work does not have to control your time. It's your prioritized to-do lists that should drive your schedule—not your email, not your phone, not even administrators or colleagues. Stick to the planned work and respond to other requests when you're done with the priorities you've set.

Use your prioritized list system to plan larger goals and projects on a monthly basis

I keep the same prioritized lists for one month. At that point, I start fresh, asking myself, *What would happen if I didn't do this task?* I transfer anything important to the new month's list and let go of things that once seemed worth doing but actually weren't the best use of my time after all.

I like doing this on a monthly basis so I can think about my upcoming goals. I generally choose at least one large project that I want to handle, such as reorganizing messy cabinets, implementing a new teaching strategy that I need to research and gather materials for, or revamping my center materials.

I break that large project down into actionable steps and enter them in my prioritized to-do list for the upcoming month. For example, if I want to set up a book check-out system so kids can bring books home to read, I'll write down tasks like *figure out sign-out system, create sign-out sheet, find bin/rack for displaying books,* and *teach kids how to use system.* Those tasks would go under high or medium priority, depending on how anxious I am to get the system going.

I'd then write *find more books for check out* and *create system for kids to share book recommendations* under the next level down of priority, probably under "low." Those accomplishments would be great, but they're not essential to the system running smoothly and the other stuff needs to get done first.

Each morning throughout the month, I'd write down any urgent tasks on my daily to-do list and find places in the day where I can squeeze in the book check-out tasks. I'd cross them off the prioritized list and write them in on the daily list. If they didn't get done, they'd get moved to the next day's list or put back on the prioritized list.

Respond to interruptions while still making planned work the priority

When you get interrupted by unplanned work that needs immediate attention or is easier to handle right in the moment, take a few seconds to write down your next actionable step for your planned work before responding to the interruption. This will make it easier for you to pick back up where you left off.

For example, if you are typing an email before school and the school psychologist stops by to quickly fill you in on a student's issue, don't leave the email half done and take the chance of losing it accidentally or forgetting to send it. Say, "Sure, can you give me one second?" and hit save, then scrawl on your to-do list "email Sara's mom."

That will take less than 10 seconds and is no inconvenience whatsoever to the psychologist. Without being rude in any way, it sends a clear message that if she chooses to stop by unannounced, she can expect to find you diligently working on something important (which will decrease the likelihood of future unplanned visits.) Best of all, when the psychologist leaves, you can immediately refocus on what you were doing without wasting time wondering, *Now what was I doing again?*

Group similar tasks together and avoid multi-tasking

Have you noticed how much quicker it is to grade the last few papers in a stack than it is to grade the first few? That's because you get into a flow after awhile. You recognize the answer patterns, and your brain is trained on what to look for.

For that reason, it's better to grade all the papers for an assignment at once, rather than just get to a couple whenever you can. It's also more efficient to respond to all of your emails at a designated time rather than answering them one by one as they come in.

Always try to group similar tasks together. Do all your photocopies for the week in one trip to the office. Make all your parent phone calls before Open House in a single evening. Search online for multiple activity ideas at once. Get your brain in a productive flow, and go with it!

Multitasking is often the enemy of productivity, because our brains just don't switch between tasks as well as we'd like to think they do. Every time we stop grading papers to look at a notification message on our phones, we lose precious seconds as our brain registers the notification, reads the subject line, processes the information, decides whether to respond or not, and so on. We then lose more time when we return to the grading, having to re-read to find out where we were at and shift back into the mindset for grading.

When you multi-task like this, each individual task takes longer to complete than if you'd gotten into a grading flow and concentrated solely on that, and then gotten into a messaging flow and concentrated on that. So, figure out what's most important, do that task (and any similar tasks) first, and then move on completely to the next thing on your list.

Trust that you will have the motivation to complete low priority tasks eventually

This has been one of the hardest principles for me to internalize personally, because it requires a great deal of faith in one's self. We have to trust that the inspiration and motivation to do low priority tasks will surface eventually, and we have to let go of the self-imposed pressure we create in the meanwhile.

For example, one year I moved to a new classroom where the math manipulatives were a complete mess. All the pieces were mixed up and there was no organizational system. I wanted to put all the like pieces together instead of having individual bags for each student, but I knew that redoing the system would take at least 2 hours, and I just couldn't bring myself to get started.

I wrote on the low priority section of my to-do list "Reorganize math manips." Every time we used the manipulatives in class, I inwardly cringed, but reminded myself, *Don't stress. It's on the to-do list, so it will get done eventually. My students will not stop learning and the world will not end if I haven't yet created the perfect organizational system.*

One day in October, a co-worker that I carpooled with called and whispered anxiously that she had a last-minute meeting that was probably going to take quite a while, considering that an entire team of attorneys had just stormed into the principal's office. I knew I was stuck at school for a good hour or more, and my eyes went immediately to those math manipulatives. *Today was the day.*

I worked quickly and with single-minded focus, knowing that my colleague could show up at any minute and I'd have to stop whether the task was finished or not. I grouped all the similar tasks together so I could get in a flow: first all the sorting, then all the labeling, and so on. The time flew by, and before I knew it, a task that had been hanging over my head was finished…and it felt great.

When you accomplish something you've been putting off or dreading, take a moment to acknowledge that. Build faith in yourself that you can do hard and unpleasant things. Then when you start to think you will never get through your entire to-do list, you can remind yourself: *I have a history of doing hard things. I've done X, and Y, and Z! I will get to this task eventually. There's no reason to worry. I can trust myself.*

Make your to-do list feel meaningful and celebrate your accomplishments

If there is something boring, stressful, or pointless you are required to do, knock it out but don't dwell on it. This advice applies before, during, and after the process.

For example, if you know you'll need to spend an hour this week entering assessment data into a spreadsheet, don't think about it constantly or complain to others that you still haven't done it. This creates a sense of dread that is out of proportion to the task. Just write it on your to-do list or schedule it into a timeslot on your calendar, and then choose to focus your thoughts on other things.

When the time arrives for you to enter the data, make the experience as pleasant as possible. Sit someplace comfortable, and turn on ambient lighting and/or background music that you enjoy. You can even set up a reward for yourself: *When I finish this, I'm going to spend as long as I want chatting online with friends or get a meal I love from my favorite restaurant.* Reject unproductive thoughts like, *I can't believe I have to do this. It's so stupid. What a waste of time.* That only raises your stress level and makes the task more unpleasant.

After you're done, don't rush on to the next task or think about how you're going to have to do the same thing all over again next week. Create a sense of accomplishment and pride in your work! Celebrate yourself the same way you'd celebrate a student who persevered through a dreaded task: *Great work! You got it done, it was accurate, and you didn't waste time getting upset or protesting. That was a huge accomplishment today.*

It's also helpful to infuse meaning into mindless tasks. File your paperwork while listening to an inspiring podcast or energizing music. Set up your science materials while daydreaming new ways to teach a physics concept. Change your hallway bulletin board display at the same time as your colleague next door and brainstorm teaching strategies together.

When in doubt, choose the kids

You'll notice that the examples I've given of interruptions and unplanned tasks that need to be delayed have nothing to do with your time spent teaching and connecting with kids. All the planning and scheduling is meant to control the other demands on your time—email, grading, paperwork, etc.—so that you are better able to focus on your students in class. That is your number one job.

We have a tendency to get overworked and think that our lesson or our goal of getting kids to meet learning standards is the most important thing, and the kids' needs become an interruption. The opposite is actually true: the kids are the most important thing, and the work is secondary. You teach students, not standards.

Whenever you are unsure of your priorities or unable to make a decision about how to use your time, ask yourself, *Which of these tasks will benefit students the most?* and dedicate more energy to those tasks. You can always feel good about time you spend helping kids and meeting their needs.

5

Go the extra mile for families (but don't take forever to get there)

I think it goes without saying that if you have good relationships with your students' families, your job as a teacher becomes infinitely more enjoyable and less stressful. After all, it's incredibly de-motivating to have your every move questioned by parents, spend hours conferring via email and phone on minor issues, or constantly chase parents down to get a form signed.

And yet those interactions are often the extent of our relationships with students' families…if we manage to spend more than a few minutes a month communicating with any one parent at all. Meeting the kids' needs is more than a full time job, and we just don't have the time and energy to reach out to parents beyond the required conferences and back-to-school events. We tend to provide the very basics of communication in hopes that parents will do their jobs and leave us alone to do ours.

But what if there were some ways to connect with and actually enjoy your students' families? What if you could work together as a team to accomplish goals, and sometimes step out of your respective roles to celebrate the kids in a fun way?

Imagine how those experiences could impact the quality and tone of the conferences you hold later in the year. How much more confident would you feel about approaching a parent with a problem if you'd already built a solid rapport and knew the parent genuinely liked and respected you?

In this chapter, I'll share some lessons I've learned about building relationships with students' families while still prioritizing the time I have with my own family. I believe it is possible to go the extra mile for families in your community without taking forever to get there— meaning you can choose a handful of communication tools and outreach methods that make a huge impact without a huge time commitment.

Get parents on your side from day one (or even earlier)

If you want to build a strong rapport, you need to make a strong first impression. You never want your initial contact with a parent to be centered around a problem. And since some kids will present serious issues on the very first day of school, the sooner you can establish contact, the better!

I know some teachers who send out letters or eCards before school begins in order to introduce themselves, welcome the kids to class, and let parents know how to reach them via email. Kids love getting mail from their teacher, and it really sets a positive, reassuring, and welcoming tone for the year.

For me, it was nearly impossible to contact students or families in advance because I never had access to a final class list until the first day of school. So, my initial contact was always on the first day when I made a phone call home to every parent. I know that sounds ridiculously time-consuming, but hear me out: the time you spend calling parents on day one could end up being the most important hour of your entire school year.

The call itself can be short and sweet: introduce yourself, tell the parent how their child's first day of school went (this is especially important for elementary school students), ask if they have any questions…and most importantly, *say something nice about their child.* It's even more effective if you can remember a specific detail about the student's personality or interests. End the call by telling the parent outright, "I love teaching this grade level, and I'm excited to have your child in my class. Contact me anytime."

Usually your call will go straight to voicemail, either because the parents aren't available to talk in the middle of the afternoon or because they don't recognize the number you're calling from. That's fine and it will save you time. I usually left a message like this:

"Hi, this is Mrs. Watson. I'm ___'s third grade teacher this year. I just wanted to introduce myself and tell you I'm really happy to have ___ in my class this year. She had a great first day and seems like a really sweet/funny/smart/outgoing girl. I'm looking forward to getting to know her and you all better. If you have any questions for me at any time, the best way to reach me is via email at ___, or you can call the school and leave a voicemail. I hope to meet you at Open House at 7 pm on Sept. 3. Have a wonderful evening and tell ___ I'll see her tomorrow morning."

In total, it usually took me just over an hour to reach out to the families of every child in my class. That's a very small amount of time to communicate the following on an individual basis:

- The first day went smoothly (addressing a big worry for many parents of younger students, especially.)
- I like your child and am taking time to get to know him/her.

- I enjoy my job and am excited about teaching.
- I am easy to get ahold of and will be responsive to your needs.

Another huge advantage to calling parents right away is that you'll know who hasn't given you a working phone number before you actually need to contact someone. I once had a student who was suspended for assault on the second day of school. What a relief to know that I had a reliable way to get ahold of the parent and had already established contact and communicated my acceptance of the child.

I'll warn you that some parents will think it's strange that you're calling them basically to say hello. They won't understand the reasoning and won't have anything to say to you. That's okay! Most parents have never received a call from school unless there was an emergency or their child was in trouble, and they might not know how to respond to a teacher who calls simply to make them feel welcome and valued. You're not responsible for how they receive and interpret your call; you're only responsible for doing your part to establish a connection.

Know and celebrate your community

One of the highlights of my entire educational career was during my third year of teaching, on the day my pre-kindergarten kids "graduated" to kindergarten. I managed to get permission to hold the celebration in a park next to the school and intended to make it a very special day.

I planned the event with the school's family service worker and a group of parent volunteers, most of whom were Nigerian or Ghanaian. During our initial meeting, I asked them whether we should use the grill in the park to cook hamburgers and hot dogs.

One of the moms asked in a sweet, tentative tone, "Would it be okay with you if we brought Nigerian food, too?"

I froze, realizing immediately that I'd made a rookie mistake. I'd had my own vision of what the celebration should look like and was about to shoehorn my kids' families into it, instead of creating a shared vision based on the community I was serving. Fortunately, it wasn't too late—you should have seen her face light up when I told her that I would love for the families to bring their favorite dishes to the potluck.

On the day of graduation, the kids performed and had their ceremony in the park, and let me tell you, we had a *feast* afterwards. I had a small boom box and a CD of kid-appropriate music to play, but one of the dads asked if he could pull his SUV up to the picnic area and play music through the vehicle's sound system: "We have Ghanaian music, would it be alright to play it? *Really*—it is okay? We can play it?" I smiled and assured him that I would love to hear Ghanaian music.

That year, graduation looked nothing like I would have planned it. But it was the best feeling to look around that park at the families enjoying their kids, listening to some of the most beautiful music I've ever heard, and eating delicious foods that were special to my families. I liked the music so much that I asked the parent to burn me a copy of the CD—I thought he was going to cry, he was so excited to hear that I liked his music. I still picture that scene in my mind, and it makes my heart sing.

That experience bonded us together as a class. It let the parents meet the kids that their own children talked about all the time, and allowed them to forge relationships with other parents so the kids' friendships could blossom outside of school. And I don't think I can overstate how much the experience endeared me to those families as they saw me embrace them and their cultures with open arms, and love on their kids like they were my own. Nor can I overstate the impact it had on me as I learned what makes my students' families unique and saw how they interacted apart from the school environment. I was incredibly sad to end the school year and wished I had attempted a gathering like that earlier on.

Hold monthly or quarterly Family Festivities

The effect was so profound that the following school year when I taught third grade, I started holding family events every month, starting at the very beginning of the school year, so that we had a chance to bond and get to know one another informally. Parents got to see me interacting with the kids in natural ways rather than just in the task-driven teacher role I held during the school day, and they could see firsthand that I genuinely cared about their kids.

I sent home a schedule of events at the beginning of the school year so parents could mark their calendars. One month, we had a Math Family Festivity and the kids showed their parents how to play the math games we learned in class. Another month we held a poetry reading. Yet another month was a holiday celebration and the students showed off what they had learned in social studies about traditions around the world.

These were very simple events held either on the night of another special event at school (when I knew that co-workers, admin, and security officers would be present) or first thing in the morning. Over time, I started to realize that the early morning events were the easiest for me because I only had to come in an hour early, rather than stay several hours late.

Some of the best-attended family festivities were just 30 minutes long, held from 7:15-7:45 am, with all the adults cleared out of the room in time for the first bell to ring at 8:00 am. Volunteers would bring coffee and breakfast, and I'd create time for socialization as well as learning activities. It set a great tone for the day, and I loved seeing the families develop relationships not only with me, but with each other, too. You can read more specifics about these Family Festivities at unshakeablebook.com.

Share good news from school

Not every family outreach method has to be complex or involved. An easy way to encourage positive communication with families is to occasionally share great things their kids are doing in class.

I designed some postcards called "Good News from School" which you can download for free from unshakeablebook.com. I sent the image files to an online printing service I had a coupon for, and got a stack of 100 (three year's worth!) for around $10.

At the beginning of the year, I addressed one postcard to each child in the class. I then selected one postcard each week and wrote a quick note on the back to share something great the child had been doing in school.

During the years my school agreed to pay for postage, I mailed the postcard, and during the other years, I sent it home in the child's backpack. Because the cards were pre-addressed, they only took a few minutes to write, and I could easily see which students hadn't yet received one. If a student transferred to a different school before I had a chance to send his or her postcard, I used it a week or so after the transfer to let the student know we missed him or her.

In many cases, an email or eCard would work just as well. However, if you think your families might enjoy displaying the postcard on their refrigerator or want to save it for a scrapbook, it might be worth the extra energy to send a postcard. If kids know this is a tradition you follow, they'll anxiously await the time when it's their turn to receive mail.

Establish ongoing two-way communication

If you've ever undergone the National Board Certification process, the "ongoing two-way communication" phrase is one that's been drilled into your head endlessly during the months you worked on Entry 4. I had never heard of it until applying to be an NBCT, but learning about ongoing two-way communication created a transformational shift in the way I communicated with families. I learned that it's not enough to keep parents informed about what's happening in the classroom; you also need to provide parents with opportunities to share information with you.

There are lots of different formats this two-way communication can take. In my early days of teaching, we used to have home-school journals in which I would write notes to parents and they could write back. Over the years, our communication improved with technology. "Remind" is a great free tool/app because you can send voicemail messages and audio reminders to families (and allow them to respond back) without giving out your cell phone number.

You can also create a class blog for two-way communication. There are lots of free sites that allow you to set up a password-protected blog in minutes. You can write quick updates on what kids are learning, share student work, post pictures, and have students take turns authoring posts. You can also use appropriate social media resources for these purposes. I recommend Edmodo, which functions similarly to Facebook but is designed for schools.

Encourage families to leave comments on the blog or social media account you've created for the class. They can even offer to guest post if they have homework or test prep tips, ideas for fun educational activities over school breaks, and so on. Or, post similar topics as questions for parents to answer, and invite them to leave a comment with their favorite holiday photos, local kids' events, and so on.

You should know up front that some parents won't take advantage of these opportunities—don't become discouraged by their lack of participation. You can't allow students who won't participate in a lesson to derail your enthusiasm, and you can't allow non-responsive parents to do that, either. As you continue to share information and invite families to share throughout the school year, you can feel satisfied with knowing that you've done your part.

Be pro-active with demanding parents

Do everything you can to contribute to a good working relationship with your students' parents. Thinking that you don't have the time or energy to do this is just going to make your job harder and more unpleasant. Learn which parents want updates on everything, and be sure to keep them in the loop as much as possible.

If you just *know* you are going to get a phone call about something, don't sit around and fume about it! Head that parent off at the pass with a note or phone call to explain your side of the story before any misunderstandings occur.

You don't have to sit around passively, waiting for your daily email from a "helicopter parent" demanding information or accommodations, and then scramble around to try to pacify them. Take the lead, and call the parent in for a conference and set up a workable system that both of you can agree on. Figure out exactly what they want from you, provide as much of that as possible, and draw firm boundaries around the things you're unable to do so they'll stop asking.

When parents seem to think of a new request every day, offer to set up a standing conference time or informational session once a month to discuss upcoming projects or units of study and address any questions the parents might have. Many times, the real issue for micromanaging, hyper-critical parents is fear: they are afraid of not having control over their child's life, and are afraid their child might not get the absolute best possible education.

So in every interaction, try to alleviate those fears by giving the parent lots of information up front and the chance to ask questions, make suggestions, and request accommodations. I've found it's much less stressful and time consuming—both for me and for the parents—if I provide time for these discussions in advance, rather than handling every issue day by day as it arises.

Showing the parent you are taking his or her concerns seriously, doing everything you can to meet the child's needs, and are willing to confer about progress on a regular basis will work wonders— especially if you do it with a genuinely positive attitude.

Be pro-active with uninvolved parents

Being pro-active is also the solution for parents who don't interact with you enough. If you know certain parents aren't going to return a form or show up to a meeting, figure out how you can set them up for success. Don't be that teacher who sends home a single note while mumbling, "She's never going to read this" and then runs off to the staff lounge to complain about how uninvolved students' parents are. Instead, have some extra copies of notices already run off and be prepared to send them home again without getting upset about it.

I've found it's easier to have a good attitude about the extra work that comes with supporting parents by reminding myself of all the times *I've* needed additional reminders, have forgotten dates, or lost important paperwork.

For example, I've been pretty bad about completing and returning important tax documents to my accountant. Opening my mailbox to find an envelope stuffed with papers written in legalese feels overwhelming and intimidating to me, and so I procrastinate in handling it.

But my accountant never gave me a hard time or guilt trip about it. Instead, he started sending me copies of the forms with important information highlighted and little stickers that show me exactly where to sign. He even includes a stamped, self-addressed envelope to increase the chances that I will get the documents back to him quickly.

I assure you this is much more effective than if he'd sent passive aggressive reminders and sat around fuming to himself, "How hard is it just to fill out some forms and send them back? These are important documents! All my other clients return their forms on time. If Angela won't sign, then fine, it's her loss!"

It sounds kind of silly when you apply the situation to someone else, doesn't it? The truth is that anytime you make a request simpler and faster for someone else to complete—and you do it without acting like it's a gigantic inconvenience—you're going to have a greater chance of getting the result you want.

If you're a very conscientious person who rarely has problems returning forms or showing up on time for meetings, use those strengths to help parents who struggle. Think about what procedures you put in place that make you so successful with organization and time management, and try to set up those procedures for students and parents, as well.

Adopt an attitude of grace toward students' families

Be kind and welcoming whenever a parent makes an effort to support their kids' education, even if it's not the type or quality of support you'd prefer.

If you don't meet a certain parent until he shows up for an end-of-year event, what purpose does it serve to give him the cold shoulder or remind him of all the events he missed? Just smile and tell him how happy you are that he made it.

If a parent sends you 10 different websites with research on improving the way you teach writing, how is it helpful to get defensive and tell everyone you know how rude the parent was to question your methodology? Tell her thank you, and check out the links. Who knows, she might have saved you a lot of time in looking for great new teaching ideas!

We have no idea what struggles people have behind closed doors. We also don't know their perception of school: many of our students' parents were told they were failures or had other extremely negative experiences when they were students, and school is an uncomfortable place for them to be. Other parents may have had bad run-ins with their child's other teachers and are extremely wary of trusting you. Although you can't undo that damage and are not responsible for it, you can create a positive experience for parents in the present moment.

Remember, the objective here is to enjoy teaching every day. It is not to teach parents a lesson or make people behave the way they "ought to." You can fight a battle without letting it consume you mentally, and you can also let things go for the sake of having peace. Sometimes the choice is to be right or to have a right relationship with someone else, and it's worth considering which one is the case for you.

Accept the fact that some parents will never, ever like you

I think this is a really important point to include here, because there will be some people in life that you can never please. Sometimes it's a personality conflict, and sometimes the person has their own issues that they project onto others. Almost every year, I had a parent who seemed determined to find fault with my performance, and I used to find it extremely demoralizing. I would beat myself up about it, thinking if only I was a better teacher, all the parents would like me.

It took me years to figure out that it's pretty normal for teachers to have at least one parent every year who cusses at them, micro-manages and constantly questions them, goes over their head to the principal about a minor issue, or disrespects them in a myriad of subtle or not-so-subtle ways. Be mentally prepared for that and don't take it personally! This happens to *every* teacher, whether or not they tell the world about it.

Don't let negative parents get you so discouraged that you stop trying to build rapport with everyone else. Don't punish all the other parents because one or two of them are impossible to please. You must choose not to let a handful of parents steal your joy and enthusiasm for teaching, because there are many other families depending on you.

Never give up and always keep pushing to make parents your allies

Parents are less likely to assume the worst about you when they received an initial welcome phone call on the first day of school, find "good news from school" postcards in the mail, and have been invited to a special Family Festivity every month so they can see your classroom in action and feel like they're a part of it. And that one parent whom you can't seem to please will find it much harder to drum up support for her position or turn the other parents against you when the families have had a chance to get to know and like you as a person.

So, keep reaching out to your most challenging parents and document every attempt at communication. You always want to look back and know that you truly gave your all, feeling confident that any rifts in the relationship didn't stem from a lack of effort on your part.

Make parents feel like an integral part of the learning process and provide opportunities for them to contribute in ways that are comfortable and meaningful. Concentrate on getting to know parents as individuals, and you will be amazed at the wealth of resources and life experiences they bring to your classroom community.

6

Learn to say "no" without guilt and make your "yes" really count

There is so much behind-the-scenes work happening in schools, from tracking bus arrivals in the morning to staying late with kids who weren't picked up at dismissal; from organizing assemblies to managing after-school tutoring sessions. With all the budget cuts most schools are facing, these kinds of tasks are increasingly falling to teachers, generally without pay.

In most cases, 20% of the staff does 80% of these crucial tasks that keep the building running smoothly. I'm sure you can immediately think of the people in your school who do the lion's share: arriving at the crack of dawn, leaving at sundown, and often heading over to the building on weekends, too.

Thank God for those people. Our schools would fall apart without them. Show them support. Express your gratitude. Do little things to make their jobs easier.

But you don't have *become* one of them.

I sincerely applaud the teachers who enjoy devoting most of their free time to school stuff. I've gone through periods in my life like that, and I think it's great to see teachers spending so many hours devoted to projects they're passionate about. If you can relate, please don't let me dissuade you from the fantastic, important work you're doing!

This chapter is for teachers who are in a different season of their lives. This is for the teachers who work far more hours than they want to and desperately need more time for family and other priorities. It's also for the teachers who get trapped into taking on responsibilities they don't enjoy and who wish they could say "no" more often.

The tips that follow will help you choose your commitments wisely and establish boundaries with colleagues, administrators, and students' parents.

Clearly communicate your policies to parents

Before the school year begins, it's important to plan out your grading criteria, homework expectations, policies for accepting late work, response to tardiness, and so on. These don't need to be hard and fast rules for which you can never make an exception, just a general outline of your approach to various situations.

When will you typically be available for conferences? How much time can you allot in an average week to helping students after school? Will you provide make-up work for unexcused absences? How quickly can students expect to have assignments returned?

Planning your policies out in advance will help you think critically about the ways you can and cannot reasonably accommodate others. It allows you to thoughtfully consider how you will respond to infractions and unreasonable requests so that you don't make a rash, emotional decision during a conflict. If you want other people to respect your time, you must be clear on what they can and cannot expect from you.

If possible, decide on policies together with your grade level team and get everything approved by administration. This will provide consistency among the various classrooms (since parents do compare notes) and lend authority to your policies if a parent accuses you of being unfair.

Type everything up in plain language to create a class handbook and have students and parents sign a form agreeing to your policies at the beginning of the school year. I sent mine home (and provided a link to the class website where my policies were posted) the week before Open House. I let parents know I welcomed their questions individually through phone calls and email, and explained that I would clarify all policies when I met them at Open House. The signed form served as proof that each family had received my policies and agreed to them.

I found that about 95% of students and parents were respectful of my policies when they knew everything up front and understood the reasons why the policies were in place. The remaining 5% would probably not have been agreeable to any rules or consequences I tried to enforce, so I handled them on a case-by-case basis. Working with the more challenging kids and parents was definitely easier when I knew that everyone else was on my side and clear about my expectations.

Tactfully enforce boundaries for parent communication

I usually had a handful of parents who picked up their kids after school and wanted to hold impromptu conferences, and I had no problem with them stopping me briefly with quick questions. However, sometimes parents would take advantage and pull me into long, unnecessary conversations about family situations, or try to corner me into discussing the minutiae of our school day for twenty minutes every afternoon.

Normally I would just switch up my routines so that I wasn't in a predictable location or had to leave the drop-off area immediately due to other obligations. If that failed, I got a little more direct and said, "I'm glad you brought this up—we really should talk about it when I'm able to give you my full attention. Can we schedule a conference later in the week?" Most of the time, the parent decided the topic wasn't important enough to warrant the lengthy discussion they'd inadvertently started, and realized that I had other tasks to attend to after school.

If you have parents with whom it's difficult to wrap up any conversation, I recommend scheduling conferences *before* school. This way, the discussion will come to a natural end as soon as students can be heard lining up outside the room. If the parent needs to meet with you after school, try to schedule another parent conference immediately afterward so there's someone waiting at the door.

If you have parents who send you emails all day long, you might find it helpful to use an auto-responder message: *Thanks for your email. I'm working with students for most of the day, but I wanted you to know I have received your message and will respond to it after the kids have gone home.* I don't like to set the precedent that I respond to non-urgent emails during the school day, and try to teach parents not to expect a reply until late afternoon or evening. Because they know they won't get a reply during instructional time, many times parents will call the school secretary for information instead.

I've experimented with various policies about parents contacting me after school hours. One year, I gave out my cell number and took calls anytime. Another year, I didn't give it out and refused to even look at email until Monday morning. Neither system worked well for me, and I discovered that I prefer to take things case by case, since some parents need more boundaries, whereas others have very special situations that deserve more flexibility. Using a free tool like Google Voice can allow you to communicate with certain parents via a voicemail message after hours without giving out your home or cell phone number.

Don't make "no" your default reaction

I went through a phase as a new teacher in which I refused to budge an inch with my students' families. I believed it was best to have stringent policies about how I would and would not accommodate their needs, and then apply those policies across the board. My theory was that any exceptions would create accusations of unfairness or lead to parents taking advantage of me.

One day, a mother showed up at 3:05 pm for a 2:30 conference, arriving after teachers' contractual hours for the day were over. I asked the more experienced teacher next door if I should hold the conference or not. "It's after hours," she replied flatly. "If you do it this time, you'll have to do it every time." So, I told the school secretary to let the parent know I was not available.

The following morning when I arrived at school, the secretary said to me, "I thought Mrs. Juarez was going to cry when I told her she couldn't see you. You know she and her husband just moved here and they both work two jobs, right? She had 20 minutes in between shifts and this was the only time she could make it. She said she doesn't know when she'll be able to come back in."

My heart sank.

I never did meet that child's parents, not the whole year. They were very active in their daughter's education, always making sure her homework was completed and forms were signed and returned. But I had either squandered the one chance this parent had to meet with me, or turned her off so much with my inflexibility that she never bothered to try again.

If I could redo that day, I'd say, "I'm on my way out of the building now. I have an appointment at 3:30 [with my couch], so I can't stay long. But I'll be happy to meet with you in the office for a few minutes to talk about your daughter's progress."

That would have sent a clear message to the parent that I'm not available at all hours, and if she's late, she's going to get stuck with a very abbreviated meeting. But the response is also respectful of the fact that she cared enough about her daughter's education to come over to the school and talk with me—something that a lot of parents never do. Staying after school for 10 measly minutes in order to meet with this parent would have been no big deal, and I wouldn't hesitate to do it today.

Individualize your communication with parents

A stay-at-home mom, a high-powered attorney mom with a nanny, and a single dad working three jobs are probably going to need different things from their kids' teachers. And yet most of the time, we don't individualize our communication or outreach to families. Frustration sets in as we expect all parents to provide the same type and quality of communication with us (and the same level of learning support at home.) That's just not realistic!

Communicating with all parents in the exact same way is like teaching kids with different learning styles and ability levels using the exact same lesson: sometimes it's necessary, but it's always more helpful to accommodate their weaknesses and play to their strengths. The end goal is the same for everyone, but you can adapt and differentiate what you do to get there.

For example, I once had a student whose parents were going through a bitter divorce. The father accused the mother of deliberately withholding information about their son's progress in school. He came in for a conference and asked me to mail to him a copy of all the school's newsletters and fliers plus all the notes and behavior/academic growth reports that I sent home.

When he first asked, I immediately bristled, knowing the request would definitely require extra work on my part. I had no desire to set the precedent of making extra copies and mailing them out whenever parents asked. But I quickly stepped back and looked at the big picture view: this was a father who loved his son and wanted to be involved in the child's life despite seeing him only twice per month. He was trying to initiate regular communication with me—something I worked tirelessly and unsuccessfully to achieve with many other parents.

So, I told him yes. I asked for a stack of self-addressed, stamped envelopes so I could minimize my time and expense, and the father gladly provided them. I notified the school secretary that I would now need 29 copies of all flyers instead of 28. I already had a "mailbox" system set up in my classroom so that each child had a slot for papers to go home, and I simply created an extra slot for this child. Each Friday, I asked the student to take out the papers in his first slot and put them in his backpack for mom, and take out the papers in the second slot and put them in one of the envelopes for dad so I could mail it off. It was that simple!

Accommodate special requests but emphasize your policies

Every relationship involves give and take. If permitting a request will make a child's parents feel more comfortable and put them on your side instead of pitted against you, just do it!

It's okay, for example, to send one family a daily email on their child's behavior and not do that for all of your students. Your job is not to treat everyone equally, but to treat them equitably. You don't have to announce to anyone else that you're making an exception: just do what it takes to support that student and her family.

The key is to make it clear to the parent that your policy still stands and this is a one-time or short-term exception that should be kept confidential. You can say, "I don't normally ___. Just between you and me...I'm making an exception in this case because I really believe it's in the best interests of your child and I want to help you guys out." This frames your accommodation as a very special favor, and can generate a lot of good will if you say it with kindness and not from a power trip!

If you're afraid the parent will take a mile if you give an inch, say, "I think it makes sense for me to allow ___ this time, but I want to be clear that in most circumstances, my policy is still ___. I want to be as consistent as possible with following the established policies, especially since those are the expectations my principal has approved. I really appreciate your support with this."

Make your "no" feel like a compromise to parents

There will be times when parents' requests are truly unreasonable or unfeasible. For the sake of the relationship, it's important that you communicate your "no" without showing an attitude of *how dare you ask me to do that*. In fact, the parent should walk away from the conversation feeling like she or he was granted at least a portion of what was requested.

My personal response to inappropriate requests is to meet with parents and tell them I view us as a team of equal partners who need to create an understanding of how to move forward. Sure, it's *my* classroom, but it's *their* child. Many parents are resentful of the authority that school holds over their children's lives (decreeing what learning standards must be met by which date, how much work must be completed at home and when, etc.) The perceived power imbalance makes them get irrationally angry.

I start off by telling the parents that we are on the same side: we both want what's best for their child, and now we simply need to figure out what that "best" will look like in this situation. I explain my position and rationale, and allow the parents to explain theirs.

Then I say, "I want to propose a solution. Neither of us will be 100% happy with it, but I hope we can both agree to compromise a little bit and meet in the middle. What if we ___? Could that work for you?" If we can't compromise or I'm truly unable to budge from the policy, I'll usually invite an administrator to attend a follow-up meeting so she or he can back me up or authorize a policy exception.

Remember, the idea here is to learn how to say "no" and make your "yes" really count. Give in on the things that make a big difference to parents but aren't a huge deal to you. Be a little more flexible than you'd like in some circumstances so that you can give a firm "no" in a more important circumstance.

Choose high impact school commitments

As you practice setting healthy limits on what you're willing to do, aim for the types of family outreach, committee work, and other commitments that give you the biggest return for your time investment.

I have a friend who agreed to run the science fair at her school. It's a massive project that consumes her life for 2 months each year. But, she really loves the science fair. She's passionate about hands-on science investigations and fostering kids' curiosity about their world. It's exciting to her that the whole school participates and she gets to support the learning of 800 kids instead of just her 25.

Because it's such a big responsibility, the science fair has become an important leverage tool which helps her guard the rest of her free time. Most people know not to ask her to take on other big projects, and if someone mistakenly assumes she'll also want to run the math fair, she says, "Aw, I wish! My husband would kill me if I took on another responsibility like that. I spent so many months preparing for the science fair; I couldn't do that to my family again. I'm sorry!"

If you're going to commit to something major in your school, make sure it's something you care about and are highly motivated to do…and then stay focused on it. It's better to do one thing well than ten things halfway.

Contribute to your school community in last minute tasks

Personally, I prefer to avoid big project commitments because coordinating with a bunch of people stresses me out and leaves me with no energy for my most important job at work, which is teaching kids. So my approach is to volunteer for the small, last minute tasks that crop up on a regular basis.

If a parent on the PTA was preparing for a meeting and said she'd forgotten to make copies of the agenda, I'd say, "Oh, I'll do it for you! I can stop by the office right after school and run everything off."

If the principal made a loudspeaker announcement that the bus loop needed an extra staff member because someone went home sick, I'd call down to the office immediately and volunteer.

If a co-worker was making an important phone call during her lunch break, I'd offer to pick her students up from the cafeteria and bring them to the classroom so she could finish her conversation.

All of these tasks helped to relieve the burden and stress on other people—many of whom were busy overseeing larger efforts before and after school—and hopefully gave me the reputation of being a team player. Yet none of the tasks required any commitment on my part or more than just a few minutes of my time.

Sometimes the smallest things make the biggest difference for people, especially if those people are feeling stressed out and crunched for time. If you're too busy for big commitments, seize those smaller ones whenever possible.

Select your committee work wisely

Most schools require every staff member to be a part of at least one committee. If you're lucky, you'll get to choose which one(s) you join.

I used to choose my committees based solely on what I was interested in. After all, work is a lot more enjoyable when it's something you care about, and that principle certainly applies to committee work. But I learned the hard way that there are two other factors that are equally as important.

The first factor is how much work the committee is responsible for. A music committee might sound like fun, but if members are responsible for putting together three school-wide performances a year, you need to carefully weigh the decision to be involved. I once chose to be on a technology committee, not realizing that meant I'd be responsible for setting up the interactive whiteboard and sound equipment before every single PTA and staff meeting *and* taking it down again afterward—requiring me to come in early and stay late on a pretty regular basis.

The second factor to consider is the other people on the committee. Personally, I've found it's better to work with agreeable, easy-going, responsible co-workers on something I don't particularly like than to be committed to a mission I care about with people who are lazy, argumentative, or perfectionistic.

I try to let my co-workers choose their committees first, and then jump in once I have an idea of what the dynamics of each group will be like. Typically there are a handful of toxic personalities on staff, and I'm always very careful not to commit myself to working on anything long term with them if I can help it!

Have prepared responses that help you say "no" to additional commitments

There have been many times that I've wanted to contribute more to my school community but truly felt that taking on anything additional would be overwhelming. If someone caught me off guard and asked me to join another committee or take on more responsibility, I'd often say yes because I couldn't quickly think of an effective way to say no!

I learned to have a few ready phrases that I could draw on as needed. Often I said, "I've got more going on than usual, so if you can find someone else to do it, I'd appreciate that a lot."

Sometimes I'd add, "If you get completely stuck, let me know, and I can bail you out." I liked this approach because I knew I wouldn't have the guilt of finding out later that my co-worker stayed up until 3 a.m. doing something that I probably could have squeezed into my schedule. This strategy worked most of the time, because I clearly communicated that I should only be asked to take on the work if there was absolutely no one else who could do it, and my colleagues were very respectful of that.

In general, the best way to say no is to keep it short and sweet. Some people will use any information you give them to form a counter-argument, so the fewer reasons you give, the less leverage they have for a rebuttal.

Most of us tend to give long, drawn out explanations and effusive apologies when they're really not necessary. Resist the urge to justify yourself, and try saying:

"I'm sorry, I really need to focus on ___ right now. I hope you can find someone else who can help!"

"Oh, wow, I would love to help with that! I've got too much going on right now, but please keep me in mind next time!"

"I'm not up for that right now. Maybe you can try ___."

"I wish I could fit that in my schedule right now, but I just don't think I can make it happen. I'm sorry!"

You can also say, "I need to check with my spouse/family members on that before I commit. Can I let you know tomorrow?" That gives you time to think about the issue and talk it over with the people closest to you (which is important if the task means you'll be less available at home.) It also gives you an easy out: "Hey there, I'm sorry, I need to help my daughter with ___ and I have to leave school at 3:30 tomorrow. Maybe another time!"

If you think the "no" discussion is going to be difficult, try to have the conversation right before class starts or when you're on your way to a meeting or another obligation. Say, "I'm sorry, I can't help with that this time. I'm on my way to pick up the kids from lunch, I'll see you later!"

Soften the blow with "I can't say yes"

I recently overheard a random conversation between a JetBlue flight attendant and a passenger as our plane was taxiing away from the gate. The passenger had asked if he could get something from a bag he stowed overhead.

I expected the flight attendant to say, "No, sorry, we're taxiing, you can't get up now." That's what I would have told him! Instead she said this: "The seatbelt sign is on, so I can't say yes."

It took a moment for me to register the brilliance of that phrase: *___ so I can't say yes.* Instantly, the listener knew she was empathetic, wanted to give him what he asked for, and had a legitimate reason for not being able to acquiesce. She said no clearly and succinctly *without ever saying no.*

The possibilities for using this phrase in school are limitless. With a co-worker, you might say, "I wish I could do those lesson plans for you, but I have a meeting after school, so I can't say yes." With a parent, you could say, "I'd love to talk about that, but I can't say yes because I have another parent scheduled now." The phrases ___ *so I can't say yes* and *I can't say yes because* ___ are such a firm yet gentle way of saying no that they're effective in almost any situation.

Let go of the guilt that comes from saying no

The hardest part of setting boundaries around your time is usually the pressure you put on yourself. You feel obligated to pull your weight and genuinely want to help other people out. Sometimes you can't imagine what would happen if you said no because the impact would be so far-reaching.

So, the real battle of saying no isn't waged between yourself and others: it's in your mind. Self-imposed obligations and guilt are the biggest hurdle to overcome, and once you can make peace within yourself about the decision to say no, it becomes much easier to say it to others and truly mean it.

Train yourself to think about it this way: *each time you say yes to one thing, you're choosing to say no to something else.* There is always a trade-off with your time. You can't justify accommodating every request just because each one will only take a few minutes, because those are minutes that you must take away from something else that's important to you.

For example, if you choose to say yes to helping a co-worker after school, you're choosing to say no to planning lessons for your students, getting exercise, taking care of your personal errands, or spending time with your family. You should not feel guilty about protecting the limited time you have for those important activities!

Additionally, each yes that you give means you have less energy to devote to other areas of your life. Each new yes means the things you've already said yes to will be compromised on some level, because you have a finite amount of energy. So, consider your options carefully:

If I say yes to this new commitment, I will have less energy for the stuff I already committed to. Will I feel good about that? I might be able to squeeze in the time, but will the extra demands cause a huge drain on my energy? Which commitment is most deserving of my time, energy, and focus?

When you start to feel guilty about saying no, remember what you've effectively said yes to. Saying no to a colleague means saying yes to time for relaxing that evening. Saying no to a student's parent means saying yes to time with your own children. These are honorable, worthwhile decisions you should feel good about making from time to time.

Sometimes the right answer is yes, and sometimes it's no. Keep returning to your list of priorities and goals. If you realize that a new commitment doesn't fit into those goals, you must choose to say no to it. Time is a resource that you cannot make more of, and energy is a resource that must be carefully managed and replenished. Make thoughtful decisions about how you use your time and energy so that you can really make an impact.

7

Do your part to
create a positive school culture

A healthy work environment makes a tremendous difference in how you much enjoy teaching, and you deserve to be in a place where you feel supported and energized each day. If your school's morale is in the gutter and there is palpable tension among faculty and administrators, please know that you are not powerless over that situation, no matter how much it might feel that way.

You have the right to seek out other teaching opportunities...*and* you have the ability to influence the work environment at the school you're at right now.

Many of the suggestions I've heard for transforming school culture are top-down ideas and won't work unless administrators share the positive vision. But I believe change can come from the grassroots level, too. In this chapter, I'll share some ways that a handful of dedicated teachers can create real boosts in school morale, and ways that *one individual teacher* can improve the work environment.

You have the power to change school culture!

Don't give away your power to a toxic administrator or allow other staff members' attitudes to determine whether you enjoy your work. I have seen many instances in which teachers have banded together and thrived despite a lack of strong leadership from their administrators. I have also witnessed individual teachers bravely persevering in environments where *everyone* around them is negative.

You, personally, can have tremendous influence on your work environment if you choose to exercise it. One negative teacher can derail an entire conversation, and one positive teacher can get it back on track. One negative person can spread discouragement to everyone they see, and one positive person can spread joy and contagious enthusiasm. Your attitude is the deciding factor in how much you enjoy your work, and you have the power to impact everyone around you with the choices you make.

The number one destroyer of school morale

In my opinion, a culture of complaining is the most pervasive negative influence in schools. It starts with a handful of pessimistic teachers who only see the bad and get a kick out of telling newer teachers how much worse the school and profession have gotten over the years. Their poor attitude spreads rapidly to others who join in on the complaints under the guise of venting, being empathetic, or just fitting in. Pretty soon, it becomes the norm to turn every meeting and social gathering into a time to talk about what's wrong with students, parents, and the school system.

It's impossible to be happy during a moment in which you're complaining. Impossible. So you cannot give complaining staff members control over your conversations and you must refuse to participate in any gripe sessions. Visualize their negative words as toxic sludge and refuse to be a dumping ground for their garbage. Your mental health and enthusiasm for teaching are on the line!

You can stop the complaining cycle

If a co-worker launches into yet another tirade about the same old topic, just smile and nod, and then change the subject. You can also respond to complaints with something positive: each time someone tells a story about an irate parent or out-of-control child, share something sweet, funny, or inspiring that happened to you.

It's very annoying to chronic complainers when other people change the subject or counter with positive anecdotes, because it's no fun to whine alone. Complainers get irritated by people who continually find the good in things, so they tend to avoid optimistic personality types at all costs. That means if you're consistent with not responding or reacting to their negativity, a chronic complainer will quickly figure out that it's a waste of time to use you as their sounding board and they'll go elsewhere.

Refusing to listen to complaints means that those negative words will have no effect on you. Other teachers will be drawn to you as they witness how you manage to shut down complainers. Although it can be somewhat therapeutic for them to have someone to vent with, it is also a relief to be around a positive person who lifts them up. Other teachers will begin to seek out your company and emulate you. Over time you will influence the school culture so that complaining is no longer the norm.

Don't engage negative co-workers in any way

In team meetings, I used to try to make complainers feel heard and acknowledge their concerns. However, it can be counterproductive to validate the opinions of those who are determined to point out everything wrong with a situation and why an idea will never work.

I've found it's better to let them say their piece and then continue on with the meeting. If you're explaining a new schedule and the complainers say, "Well! That's going to make it impossible for us to teach reading groups now!" just make eye contact with them so they know you heard them, and continue explaining how the schedule will be implemented. Or say, "This will be a challenge, yes. So let's keep talking about how we can make this work" or "This is something we have to do, so let's put all our energy into figuring out a solution."

You can also wait for a pause in a person's rant and say, "Since we have about fifteen minutes left, maybe we should finish planning this out and then when we're done, we can go back and look at some of these issues that might create a problem." If your meetings are anything like mine, there won't be any time at the end and you can leave.

There's nothing you can say to convince the Debbie Downer types that a new system will be effective (especially if you're just the messenger and have doubts about it yourself), so don't waste your energy with a long back-and-forth. Always keep moving the conversation forward.

Limit your emotional investment in negative co-workers

Don't try to build friendships with complainers to stay on their good side. They will only pull you down! In fact, don't spend a minute longer than you have to with people who are rude or constantly complaining.

Prepare a mental list of things you need to get done so that you can mention one of those tasks when you pass a negative colleague in the hallway or office. Say hello and then excuse yourself by saying, "I gotta get going to make these copies before the kids come back—see you in the meeting!" You are too busy to waste time complaining, and there's no need to hide that in order to appear friendly!

You also need to be mentally and emotionally on guard around negative colleagues, especially if they have a tendency to blindside you with hurtful comments. You cannot allow yourself to take offense at passive-aggressive remarks directed toward you, because when your feelings are hurt, you can easily get sucked into an argument. Keep negative co-workers at arm's length and don't value their opinions enough to allow them to affect your feelings.

Remind yourself that rude and negative comments are usually not personal. Criticism is more of a reflection of the person who is saying it than the recipient. So if a colleague criticizes something about your teaching or tries to make you feel inferior, let it slide off your back.

Tell yourself, *This is his/her problem, and it's not about me. I refuse to allow people who dislike their job to make me dislike mine, too. I'm not permitting those rude comments to take up any more space in my mind. I'm dismissing them, and I'm replacing them now with thoughts about something that worked well in my classroom today.*

Set the tone of conversations yourself and find common interests

When you're with a group of co-workers, don't wait for someone negative to direct the flow of the discussion. Dive right into something productive and direct your comment or question to someone in the room who generally enjoys his or her job.

Say, "How did it go with that new activity you tried this morning?" or "One of my kids said the funniest thing during math today, listen to this..." or "I saw the coolest thing on Pinterest, I think we should try it!"

Talking about outside interests is another smart approach and creates a strong bond among co-workers. Share your personal lives with one another so that you can ask about families, hobbies, travels, and so on without having to revert to a clichéd, "So, did you get that stupid email from the principal?" or "You won't believe what this kid did again today" as a conversation opener.

If your co-workers don't want to share anything personal, get the ball rolling yourself by talking about something innocuous, like local restaurants ("Has anyone ever been to ___? I just tried it last week and it was really good.")

Sometimes you just don't have anything in common with colleagues, so ask the most positive (or most talkative) person in the group a question. The key here is to get someone chattering on about something that no complainer can dissuade them from. If one of your co-workers is about to have a baby, is planning a wedding, or has another exciting event happening, inquire about that. Everyone loves weddings and babies, after all. Or, ask one of the talkative teachers about what her grandkids have been up to.

It might not be the most thrilling conversational topic, but it's better than being subjected to a rant about how the entire educational system is headed down the toilet.

Share what's working and support one another's teaching

In most schools, we spend far too much time talking about what's wrong instead of recognizing what's right. You can suggest starting every staff and/or team meeting with a couple of positive anecdotes so teachers can share classroom successes. You can also talk about celebrations in your personal lives: upcoming family reunions, new home purchases, and so on. If your staff is too large to share these things as a whole group, they can share with people at their tables.

Another idea is to coordinate with your colleagues and send a weekly or monthly accomplishments email. Create a shared Google Doc or form where any staff member can quickly type in something that worked well in his or her classroom, and the person in charge just copies and pastes the text into an email or other newsletter which gets sent to the whole staff.

You can also include things you've noticed other teachers doing well, and make the email a celebration of colleagues. If you can get your PTA to purchase small gifts, a random name from the appreciation email can receive a surprise.

An even simpler idea is hang a bulletin board or dry erase board in the staff lounge and write notes about your accomplishments on it: *Sam learned 10 new sight words today! We finally finished our holiday project! I figured out a system for handling make-up work!*

Support your Sunshine Club or Social Committee

Many schools have a group of teachers who are in charge of general morale-building and social events. They send flowers when one of you is ill, plan the staff holiday party, and so on. You might not have the time to join the committee every year, but there are lots of other ways to show support.

Since the social committee is a pretty thankless job, one of the most important things you can do is let the committee members know you see their hard work and appreciate it. Don't complain about the events they organize; instead, look for things to compliment them on.

It's also important to give prompt support to the committee's requests. When they ask for a donation for someone's retirement gift, send it over right away. Show up early to events on occasion or offer to stay late and help clean up. Do whatever you can to make their job easier.

Utilize the all-purpose bonding experience…eating

It's been said that you could leave a tray of half-eaten, week old muffins in a teachers' lounge and they'd be gone in an hour. I don't doubt that one bit! Free food is a big draw for just about anyone, and sharing meals creates a bonding experience.

On paydays, try holding a Fun Food Friday in which grade level teams take turns bringing in lunch. Or, hold a potluck on the day of parent conferences to make it easier to grab something to eat during an otherwise busy evening.

Another idea is order lunch once a week (or even once a month) with other teachers who share your lunch shift. Have each person pay for his or her own, or if your group is small, take turns paying. It's even more fun to go out to lunch together on teacher workdays, or for happy hour after school on occasion.

Create fun school-wide traditions you can look forward to

Some schools do a "teacher huddle" before the first bell, gathering the staff in teams to sing the school chant each morning. Some schools put dance music on the intercom before Open House and conferences, and the staff dance together in the hallway to get energized.

Other schools offer yoga or workout sessions after school. It's rarely a formal program: a bunch of teachers just get together in a classroom or the media center, put in a DVD, and de-stress together. Once or twice a week is a good schedule, and people can drop in on whichever days they have time.

Once a month, you can have cake or other special treats at the beginning of your after-school staff meeting to honor that month's faculty birthdays. This will encourage people to be on time for the meeting and engage in some much-needed socialization for a few minutes. I know one faculty that also takes a walk together after the meeting to continue the socialization and burn off those cake calories!

"Beat the Blahs" is a really cool tradition that happens annually at my friend's school. From January through spring break, they get as many staff members as possible on board with a Beat the Blahs activity. The volunteers are divided into teams, and each team is assigned a week. During their week, they can choose any blah-beating activity they'd like: giving out little gifts, arranging a potluck or ice cream party, creating games or competitions after school, and so on.

You can also try a Teacher of the Week trophy with your entire faculty or just your grade level team. This should be done on a scheduled, rotating basis so that no one is left out. Announce at the beginning of the meeting who that week's honored teacher will be, and make small pieces of stationery or notepads available for other staff members to write encouraging messages on. Collect the notes, place them in the trophy, and at the end of the meeting, award it to the teacher.

At a small rural school I know, the staff does a "sleepover" in the nearest city right before spring break. They have dinner, go out dancing, stay in a nice hotel, and drive back to their families the following day after brunch. This creates lots of fun shared memories and really fosters a strong bond between them as a staff.

Notice that very few of these ideas require support from the school principal—they're completely teacher-directed activities that one or two staff members thought up and started doing. Even if your school leaders would never suggest one of these traditions, most of them will not stand in the way of teachers who want to quietly implement them on their own. Give it a try in your school!

Be a one person force for good

I know a teacher who surveys fellow staff members about their favorites Starbucks order, soda/juice, candy, magazines, stores for gift cards, etc. She emails this list to every staff member (you could also upload it to your school server or Google Drive for easy reference.) The school secretary keeps a copy in case parents ask for gift suggestions, and the staff members can use the list to show appreciation to each other throughout the year. Most of the items on the list cost only a few dollars, and it's money well spent since the recipient gets his or her favorite things!

I've visited a number of schools in which one or two teachers show the staff they care by sprucing up the teachers' restroom. They've added potpourri, sweet-smelling soap, picture frames, and other nice touches to make the ladies' room a place of rest and solitude. I've also seen motivational quotes hung or stenciled on the bathroom walls. Why not surprise your co-workers by planning something like this?

Another idea is to slip thank-you notes under colleague's doors, or have a student hand-deliver them as a surprise. You don't have to get fancy or spend a lot of time and money—two sentences scrawled on a sticky note are truly enough to brighten someone's mood.

Make it a goal to do this for one colleague a month and you will have encouraged ten teachers by the end of the school year. I guarantee that seeing their appreciation will put you in a great mood for the day.

I also can't overstate the impact of a verbal compliment. Because it's so rare for teachers to hear positive feedback, any kind words tend to stick in our brains and hearts forever. Make it a goal to compliment or thank one colleague a day. You might even want to take a staff roster and use it as a checklist to make sure you connect with each person.

Of course, you don't have to be alone in your quest for building school community, and it's important to find other people who will inspire and uplift you. A good support system starts by finding just one positive person that you can band together with in order to create positive change.

In the next chapter, I'll share ways to find other like-minded educators who can offer support and give you new ideas to reinvigorate your teaching and improve morale at your school.

8

Take charge of your own professional development

Teaching can start to become a boring, passionless experience when we try to teach the same lessons the same way, year after year. We can end up just going through the motions, and lose our enthusiasm because the only challenges in our day are the ones we don't want and didn't ask for.

The way to breathe new life into your teaching is to tap into your inner motivation and connect with the things, people, and ideas that matter to you. Inspiration for improving your practice doesn't just come out of nowhere: it comes from allowing your mind to drift to possibilities in your downtime, and surrounding yourself with energizing people and ideas.

If *you* don't take the initiative to increase your teaching motivation, who will?

You see, pursuing professional development is a lot like exercising. Your first thought is probably: *ugh*. After all, when you're tired, the last thing you feel like doing is heading to the gym. But if you can create routines that make working out a regular part of your life, you actually feel *more* energized afterward...and the same is true with professional development.

I know it seems totally counter-intuitive. How could something that requires so much energy expenditure actually produce more energy? But it does! And once you've established the habit, you can't imagine *not* doing it on a regular basis.

Passionate, motivated, and inspired educators don't stay that way by only attending the mandatory trainings on CPR procedures and sexual harassment prevention. They seek out learning opportunities that matter to them. They actively stir up their enthusiasm for teaching and are constantly getting new ideas for improving their practice.

But I don't want to think about school in my free time!

I'm not advocating for you to hang around the house on weekends thinking about all the problems and stressors associated with work. Don't spend your evenings rehashing that argument with a parent, stressing out about your upcoming evaluation, ranting about standardized testing, or complaining about students' behavior problems.

That's not what taking charge of your own professional development is about—not at all. It's about spending some of your free time thinking about topics you are passionate about. And hopefully, some of those topics are related to teaching and learning.

To me, taking charge of your PD is about filling your mind, soul, and spirit with things that motivate and energize you. It's about connecting with *friends*—fellow educators you enjoy talking to about personal and professional things. Self-directed PD is inherently energy giving, not energy draining.

The best PD is an opportunity YOU create

It feels like a burden when we're assigned a specific book to read or mandated to attend a professional development session. But when we choose the topics that interest us and pursue them in ways that feel natural and enjoyable, improving our practice as educators becomes something we look forward to doing.

Scrolling through my Twitter feed or Pinterest for 5 minutes a day—even if I don't feel like it—often gets me excited about my work again because I'm connecting with other people who are excited. Reading other educators' blogs motivates me to reflect on my own practice and try new things. Checking out the latest educational books gives me ideas to share with the teachers I coach and makes my job easier and more rewarding. These things inspire me to keep giving 100% in my work each day.

Taking charge of my own professional development over the years wasn't about proving that I'm on the cutting edge, ensuring students pass The Test, or labeling myself "highly effective." I just enjoy bouncing ideas off of other people and feeling like I'm not alone in the issues I'm facing. I consistently find that relying on my teacher friends increases motivation during low-energy times. Tapping into those aspects of work that I love helps me get past the parts I don't love.

Many people refer to this process as building a Personal Learning Network (PLN). This is a network of professionals you can learn and grow with informally, however you choose. In the pages that follow, I'll share a variety of different ways you can find and connect with other educators.

Initiate conversations with co-workers

Does sitting around chatting really count as professional

development? If the goal is to get re-inspired and figure out practical solutions to classroom problems, then my answer is, YES, absolutely! Informal conversations are sometimes the best PD you can have.

One night, I was feeling really discouraged about how my teaching had become so test-driven and I felt like my kids were giving up and not putting forth their best effort. I called my co-worker and within a half an hour, we came up with a tweak on my existing test practice routines that helped my kids do a total 180. Seriously!

There's nothing like talking with people who know your teaching context intimately and have seen your students in action. If you can find just one positive, innovative educator in your school, you can learn more than you ever thought possible.

You might even add a little bit of structure to make sure you have opportunities to informally collaborate on a regular basis. One year I had a particularly cohesive grade level team and suggested we meet during our lunch break every Wednesday to share best practices. We weren't very consistent with it, but at least two people would show up each week, and it was a great opportunity to get advice from people who were teaching the same standards to the same kids.

Brainstorm with other area teachers

For as long as I can remember, I've organized a get-together with my teacher friends on a monthly basis. I invite colleagues from wherever I'm currently working as well as people I've taught with previously who transferred to different schools. Often they invite friends at their new schools, and the circle widens.

We meet in the afternoon for appetizers or later in the evening for dinner on occasion. We catch up on our personal lives and compare notes about what's happening at school: *Did you hear about the new policy on ___? Has your principal asked you to ___? How are you handling ___?*

It is incredibly eye opening to discover that things you thought were only happening at your school are actually occurring on a widespread basis. I have often shared problems I was facing only to learn that a friend's school had dealt with the same thing and found an ingenious solution that I could try out immediately.

Connect with inspiring educators online

If you don't have any positive, inspiring co-workers or teacher friends nearby, that's okay. There are tens of thousands of incredible teachers sharing their ideas and supporting one another online!

Some of my very best friends are people I have met through blogging and social media. In fact, I connect with inspiring teachers all over the world on a daily basis. I have dozens of friends and thousands of acquaintances I can ask for ideas with full confidence that I'll get a helpful response right away...and they are all people who live hundreds or thousands of miles away! I would have never connected with them if it weren't for the internet.

I'm not going to sell you on the benefits of any one social media platform over another. You can develop a strong PLN through any type of social media you choose, starting with the tool(s) you like best and use most often.

What type of online activities do you already enjoy doing? Reading blogs? Surfing Pinterest? Think about how you can integrate your teaching interests into that. Look for inspiring educators to follow online in whatever form of social media you prefer.

If you're already on Facebook, join a private group for teachers to share ideas. On Twitter, there are hundreds of weekly chats to choose from. If you like Instagram, type in the commonly used teacher hashtags and see what other educators are doing.

Don't make the mistake I did when starting out and follow only people that you relate to and can commiserate with. Reading about other teachers' problems and complaints will not energize you. Instead, follow people who inspire and challenge you. Look for the people who push your thinking and see things differently than you.

Seek out a mentor—and mentor someone else

My aunt Mary is a former kindergarten teacher who understands the need for mentorship very well. She's been out of the classroom for many years, but has always enlisted the support of a life/spiritual mentor from a woman who is about 15 years older than her. The mentor was ahead of my aunt in the stages of life: she had young kids when my aunt was childless; she had middle schoolers when my aunt had little ones; she had an empty nest when my aunt had teenagers; and so on. This enabled my aunt to watch and learn from this woman's successes and failures, and talk frankly about them as she prepared for each stage of life. They've met once a week for coffee for at least thirty years. How cool is that?

The really amazing thing about my aunt Mary is that she also extends a mentor relationship to a woman who is about 15 years *younger* than her. She meets regularly with this woman, too, and helps talk her through the challenges Mary has already navigated successfully. In a few years, this woman will take on her own mentee.

I think this is a wonderful formula for creating a teacher support network. You may not be assigned a mentor by your school district, but you can develop your own informal mentor relationship with someone in your school or that you've connected with online. Find a teacher you admire who is more experienced and who has outlasted a lot of pendulum swings and changes in education, and see if you can meet even once a month to learn from his or her wisdom.

If you've got a few years of teaching under your belt already, offer to mentor a newer teacher. Don't listen to those nagging fears that you don't have anything of value to offer another educator. Never discount how much you learn during a single year of teaching! Even a second or third year teacher can have many, many valuable insights to pass on to someone who's never had their own class before.

The conversations you have as mentor and mentee don't have to be focused exclusively on schoolwork—talk about how you make time for family and relaxation, too. Just be sure to choose mentors and mentees who are generally positive about the profession, and hold one another accountable for staying focused on productive solutions. It's easy to fall into a trap of complaining and commiserating together if your mentor/mentee just wants an outlet for venting. Be very clear that you want to work with people who love teaching and who want to talk about ways to continue loving it for many more years to come.

Look for high-quality staff development events or conferences

One of the best energizers is a good teacher workshop…with emphasis on the word *good*. A high-quality professional development session will leave you dying to get back to your classroom to try out all those new ideas.

Since there's so much uninspiring PD out there, you'll need to do your homework to find the good stuff. This is when your online connections will come in very handy. You can ask your friends about local workshops that are offered, and follow the presenters online to get a feel for their style and material.

I also recommend that you seek out opportunities to attend regional, state, and national education conferences. These will broaden your perspective, give you the opportunity to hear and discuss new ideas, and allow you to connect with teachers whom you wouldn't have otherwise met.

For me, conferences are a time to meet with the educators I don't normally get to connect with apart from Twitter or Facebook. Because we talk regularly online, these face-to-face meetings are incredibly productive, and we're able to jump right into serious topics and deep problem solving. Our conversations are often the highlight of the conference for me and I learn even more than I do in the sessions!

It might be tough for you to get time off work and cover the costs of attending, but start with local or state conferences. Those tend to have cheaper registration costs, not involve as much travel, and may be held on the weekends. Give your principal lots of advance notice to find the funding and approve your leave. Make sure you offer to share what you've learned with the rest of the staff when you return!

Participate in free local Edcamps

Edcamps are a grassroots idea started and run by educators, and they're now held all over the world completely free of charge.

Here's how they work: participants show up to the event and suggest topics they'd like to talk about. Sessions are determined collaboratively and posted on a session board. During the initial opening conversation held in a main room, participants are told they can choose to attend any sessions they want, and are specifically instructed to change sessions and move around as needed to make sure they're getting PD that meets their needs.

There are 4-6 sessions which are usually just an hour each, with most of that time devoted to conversations and interactions among the participants. Edcamps don't have formal presentations, and are very participant-driven.

There's also plenty of time for networking, socializing, and sharing ideas throughout the day. The initial gathering over breakfast is usually an hour and there are often 20-30 minute breaks in between sessions so participants have time to think, share, and reflect before digging into another topic.

Some Edcamps give a generous 90 minutes for lunch (the biggest luxury of all for classroom teachers), while others do 4 sessions back to back and then end by 1 or 2 pm so participants can spend time in the afternoon continuing their conversations over a meal if they'd like. The overall effect of both types of scheduling is a relaxing, non-rushed day of PD in which informal conversations are just as valued as the actual sessions.

Edcamps are incredibly effective because they aren't just "drive-by professional development" in which tons of new information is thrown at teachers and then forgotten. The PD is actually ongoing, because there are so many online resources provided for people to share how they're implementing their new ideas and get support and feedback using the local Edcamp's hashtag on Twitter.

This "unconference" style of Edcamps is a great model for school-based staff development, too. It saves the district money because the format relies on the expertise of teaching staff rather than outsiders. Unconferences are more meaningful to teachers because you can choose the session topics offered and decide which sessions to attend.

So, how can you get involved? Search online to find an Edcamp near you, or start your own! Suggest to your administrators that they use this model for your school's next PD day. And most importantly, spread the word about these free opportunities for educators to learn and grow together.

Find and follow like-minded education bloggers

Websites and blogs have had a bigger impact on my teaching than any other form of professional development. Reading the ideas and reflections of great teachers always inspires me and keeps me motivated, and there are a few people whose blogs have totally revolutionized the way I teach.

If you're not sure where to start, figure out an aspect of teaching that lights a fire inside you—getting kids to love reading, perhaps, or creating a beautiful learning space. Then tap into that by searching online for other people who are passionate about that same topic and are sharing their thoughts about it.

Read their resources, and continue the conversation in the comments. Follow the blogger on your preferred social media platform, and participate in discussions there, too. Before you know it, you will have developed a relationship with another like-minded educator who you can share ideas with, and you'll have a go-to source of fresh inspiration you can read on a regular basis.

Choose one professional book to read each quarter or semester

The fact that you're reading this book says a lot about your commitment to the profession and eagerness to learn and grow. Many teachers don't read any books about education in their spare time, so count yourself as one of the most ambitious, even if you don't feel that way!

Most authors (myself included) run free book clubs, Twitter chats, webinars, and other online conversations about their resources. These can be a great way to reflect on what you've read and bounce ideas off other teachers. If you can't find a book study you like online, consider starting your own, or find a friend who wants to read the book and discuss it with you.

I know a group of teachers who read one book per month and get together every fourth Thursday to discuss the book. From what I hear, about 80% of the time is spent just chatting, and I think that's great. There's nothing wrong with blending your professional and personal lives.

YOU have ideas worth sharing, too!

Karen Berg once said, "When we receive without sharing, the result is stagnation...There is nothing wrong with receiving—we're supposed to receive—but if there is no sharing, then what we receive is limited and unfulfilling." I encourage you to take charge of your professional development not just with the intent to receive, but also to give.

Many teachers hear this message and think to themselves, *I don't have anything worth sharing. I don't really do anything creative or different.* But nothing could be further from the truth! Every teacher runs his or her classroom in a unique way. Everyone has something to teach someone else.

I've created my entire website, all my books, my teacher training sessions, and my curriculum resources around this principle of *simply sharing what I'm doing as an educator.* The ideas I write about are not earth shattering. But what's obvious to me is not necessarily something other people might think to try...and what's obvious to you won't come naturally to everyone else, either.

The best inventions are just small improvements on existing ideas, strategies, or products. Anytime you've taken a simple concept and tweaked it so it works better for your classroom, you've created something worth sharing. And since most teachers use very few strategies straight from the teachers' manual, it's likely that you've put your own personal spin on almost everything you do. Tell other people about it!

Don't be discouraged when someone says, "Yeah, I already do that" or "That won't work for me" because there are teachers out there who *need* your advice. Educators *need* practical solutions and there's no way we can possibly know them all. If you have solutions, share them! You never know who you might be helping to take charge of *their* own professional development.

9

Let your vision define your value and measure of success

There is an undeniable struggle right now for teachers to re-establish ourselves as the experts in education. We are under constant attack from the media and much of the general public, frequently having to defend our identity as knowledgeable, competent professionals who are worthy of respect because we contribute something of great importance to the community.

Discussions of our value center primarily on students' academic achievement as measured by standardized tests. And much of the time, we buy into that approach. After all, helping students master grade level expectations and standards is a concrete, quantifiable, and generally worthwhile outcome.

But there's a bigger problem than just the limitations of standardized tests. You see, defining our value in relation to measurable learning outcomes will eventually strip us of all autonomy.

If the focus is solely on getting kids to pass standardized tests, then why not standardize the instruction? Why do we need creative, innovative, passionate educators if we're not trying to produce creative, innovative, passionate students? If all we care about is students' mastery of tests in core academic subjects, then why empower teachers to develop their own unique teaching styles that help learners become socially adept and well-rounded?

The real reason why you are invaluable

As teachers, we need to demonstrate our value to the community in a very obvious way through our daily practice. We need to articulate and demonstrate the things that we do on a daily basis that aren't being measured by tests:

- Teach students to be open-minded as they collaborate and negotiate
- Foster empathy, compassion, and an urgent sense of social justice
- Model and demonstrate the value of hope, optimism, and risk taking
- Instill a strong work ethic so kids develop initiative and perseverance
- Provide opportunities for creativity and ingenuity
- Guide students to invent, use their imaginations, and find new solutions to real problems
- Help kids discover and follow their interests and passions

These are just a few of the practices that make teachers invaluable and indispensable. So the question becomes: are we doing them well?

Are these "21st century skills" and real life skills something we're fostering every day in our kids? Do our teaching methods take students beyond rote learning into higher-level thinking and deep, critical reflection on real issues? And just as importantly…are we conveying the value of these practices to parents and the community, or are we allowing them to think the skills measured by standardized tests are more significant?

I don't think we're ever going to get overwhelming support for these traits from people who make the big decisions in education. There are too many arguments against the human connection. The naysayers will insist that the traits are not quantifiable and testable, or that they're lacking in importance.

We have to anticipate this pushback from leaders who want to cut funds and take away teacher autonomy. Anyone who sees dollar signs as the bottom line will find a reason to frame the discussion as if students are machines that can be programmed by other machines for uniform success.

The media and public backlash against teachers comes from a sense that teachers are not worth the money that taxpayers are kicking out for our salaries. We need to show the world what we're really capable of doing for kids. We need to redefine our role so that it's obvious how much we are needed, and demonstrate how teachers (not tests) are the essential force in a school's ability to inspire children and help them connect to their world.

We have to make our teaching about more than facts and rote learning and connect to something bigger than standardized tests. We have to have a vision that is greater than student mastery of basic content. There's no time to wait for someone to mandate and regulate and fund this change…the transformation has to begin with each of us, and it has to start now.

Your worth cannot be defined by test scores

As teachers, we must consciously choose not to internalize the impossible and often contradictory messages we hear. The state and district pile more things on our plate every year without removing the old, and we dutifully take on more than is seemingly possible…and then we're told we still need to do more, and our efforts aren't good enough. In one breath, we're told our job is one of the most important on the planet, but in the next, we're told no one's going to give us the resources we need to do it well.

For these reasons and many more, you must choose to define success for yourself. Don't let a 10 minute observation determine how you feel about yourself as a teacher. Don't derive your self-worth from the scores on a test that you didn't even take yourself!

Your students' test scores can never define your value as a teacher. Your worth does not come from someone else's approval, and it does not come from how many kids you can get to pass a standardized test.

The things you do that matter most are not quantifiable. You already know this, deep within your being. So don't wait for an authority figure to tell you that. You have to be wise enough to break free from the small box you and your students have been placed in, and define success, value, and worth for yourself.

You cannot simply "do your best"

I hear a lot of teachers define success as just doing their best. They'll say, "I'm just doing the best I can do, that's all I can ask of myself."

That's not a very motivating definition of success, though, is it? And it's also not true, for one simple reason.

No one goes into the classroom and does their best every single day.

Some days you're tired. Some days you're distracted by personal issues. Some days you take shortcuts with your instruction, and some days you yell at your students. You're *not* doing your best and so you feel guilty about it.

And even on your greatest, most productive days, there are still going to be 100 items on your to-do list and there will always be other things you could have accomplished. "Your best" is good enough, but it's never going to *feel* like it's good enough.

If you define your success as a teacher this way, you will always feel like you are on a treadmill that you can't get off. You can't feel good about just doing your best at something that is so complex and that matters deeply to so many lives.

There's only one way to feel a real sense of accomplishment in your work and be unswayed by outsiders who try to define your success by numbers and data: you must have a personal vision for teaching, and work toward it with a single-minded focus.

Create a clear vision for your teaching

I remember coaching a first year teacher at an extremely challenging middle school in the Bronx borough of New York City. This poor guy knew his subject matter well but found it nearly impossible to maintain order in the classroom. He had so many topics to cover that he couldn't figure out which ones to concentrate on, and often moved forward with lessons even though the kids were paying no attention to him whatsoever.

I wanted to get back to the heart of what really mattered to him, so one day we sat down together and I asked, "Do you have a vision for your classroom?" I'll never forget the sad look on his face, the long pause, and his reluctant response: "I used to. I don't remember what it is anymore."

My friend, if you can relate to that, please don't step foot into your classroom one more day until you've given some thought to your vision. If you can't make time in your schedule to sit down and think, do it while you exercise, drive, cook, shower…whenever! Find a few moments to reconnect with the reason you entered this profession.

What really matters? What gives you a sense of purpose and accomplishment? Think big! *Why do you teach?*

Boil the answers to those questions down to a sentence or two. Maybe your vision sounds something like one of these statements:

I want to impact future generations.

I want to make a difference in the lives of troubled kids.

I want to inspire children.

I want to get kids passionate about learning.

I want to create lifelong learners.

I want to give back to my community.

I want to show the love of God to other people through service.

I want to ignite a fire in students for my subject matter.

Use your vision as your personal definition of success

Once you've figured out the right wording for your personal vision, post it somewhere so you will see it every day, either at home or school or both. Revisit it, allow it to change, and reconnect with it on a regular basis. Meditate on it at the beginning and end of the day. Return to it whenever you are discouraged or feel defined by outside sources. Your vision is what will get you through the hard times and help you feel a sense of satisfaction when no one else is saying thank you or telling you that you've done a great job.

If your vision is to make a difference in the life of a troubled kid, you can feel good about your work every day. Some days you will see a bigger impact than others, but every day becomes an opportunity to work toward your vision. Each challenge you face—no matter how frustrating or mundane or impossible—is a chance to work toward a greater purpose that matters deeply to you.

I recently had the privilege of eating lunch with a small group of incredibly passionate, dedicated educators in Milwaukee, Wisconsin. I was amazed at not only their positive attitude toward teaching, but their ability to overcome incredible odds with students in the inner city. One of the first year teachers had averaged 1.5 years of growth in her students in just the first three months of the school year!

I couldn't wait to ask them: *What is your secret for having the energy to give 100% of yourself to your job every day? How do you keep from getting discouraged and overwhelmed by all the obstacles?*

A young woman named Hannah spoke for the group. "If I don't do my job, I'm sentencing these kids to either a prison sentence or a death sentence. Without an education, most of them have no hope of a better future. That knowledge is what drives us to do what we do. It's about the vision."

These remarkable teachers understood that they are not spending their day tying shoelaces, reminding kids to put names on their papers, and filling out paperwork. *They are giving their students hope.*

Every moment of every day, they are sowing into their students' lives and giving them an opportunity for a better future. Giving 100% is not an obligation for them; it is a privilege. They are working for a higher purpose and something far beyond themselves.

Increase your energy level by tapping into your vision

Our willingness and ability to expend time and energy increases exponentially when we have a clear vision for what we're doing. Your vision can't just be a platitude that sounds good. It has to help you tap into a purpose that you believe in so strongly that you will be determined to keep going, no matter what.

A truly powerful vision will motivate you to expend more than just time. Anyone can show up physically in the classroom but not be mentally and emotionally present. Anyone can drag stacks of papers home every night and reluctantly grade them. Your vision must compel you to expend your most precious resource, *energy*. It must compel you to put your heart and soul into your work so that you get intrinsic satisfaction from completing it.

My personal vision for teaching (and for life) is to *create things that are valuable for as many other people as possible.* By nature, I am a creative person. I derive the most pleasure from life when I am creating. I get out of bed in the morning excited about the opportunity to create. I create teaching materials, I create experiences for kids and teachers, and I create words that inspire others.

I choose to view every aspect of my life as an opportunity to create. When I'm cooking, I can create a healthy meal for my family. When I'm visiting my in-laws, I can create a beautiful family bonding experience by being fully present and engaged.

Creating things of value is how I serve others and serve God. No matter how tired I am, if I view the task at hand as an opportunity to create, I can summon the energy to keep going. And because my vision for the task is so strong, *my energy is replenished by working toward it.*

Having a clear vision will help you create alignment between what you believe is important and how you act. It will increase your energy level because it lends a greater purpose to everything you do.

Don't depend on other people for recognition

Teaching is lot like parenting in that it's a pretty thankless job. For every one thing you do that gets noticed and acknowledged, there will be hundreds of other tasks that go without recognition.

If your sense of accomplishment (or even worse, self-worth) is based on receiving gold stars and back pats, I'm sorry to tell you that teaching is going to feel pretty unrewarding to you. There will be many days when you work your butt off only to have a parent accuse you of not helping their child, your principal nitpick something in an evaluation, and your students ignore you.

I have seen many teachers become completely disillusioned through dwelling on the lack of appreciation they receive. They complain constantly that no one recognizes their hard work or says thank you. Their bitterness toward parents and students who they perceive as unappreciative becomes a poison which sucks the life out of their teaching. Every task becomes pointless in their minds because "no one's going to appreciate it, anyway."

I'm not saying it's wrong to want an occasional acknowledgement. I'm saying you cannot base your happiness on whether someone else provides that for you. You cannot allow other people's actions to determine whether you feel good about your work, and recognition cannot be your primary motivation for working hard.

You must learn to reflect on and recognize your own work. Practice setting goals and rewarding yourself when you meet them. Build your personal learning network so that you have a group of educators to celebrate your accomplishments with. Don't be shy about sharing your successes with your educator friends, and help them celebrate their small wins, too.

Most importantly, you must return to your vision over and over again. It is *your* vision, no one else's, and only you will fully appreciate all of your hard work toward it.

Create a shared vision with your students

Don't forget that kids get just as frustrated with the data-driven school culture as we teachers do. Students get caught up in the drudgery of the teach-test cycle and need to connect to their own inner drive and a larger purpose. They want to be seen as more than just numbers, and want to feel like their non-tested qualities and talents matter.

Try creating a shared vision or mission statement with your class. Ask students, "What do you hope to accomplish and experience in our classroom each day? What one sentence could sum up how we want our classroom to run?" Then help them articulate a vision.

I recommend keeping your class vision brief, easy to memorize, and focused on virtues:

We will learn together and help each other become the best people we can be.
We will work hard, challenge ourselves and each other, and support one another.
We will work together to create a safe and kind community of learners.
We will respect each other, work diligently, and show enthusiasm for learning.
We will excel in all we do with compassion and integrity.
We will have fun working together and never give up on ourselves or each other.
We will strive to become independent, responsible, lifelong learners.

Post your shared vision prominently in the classroom. Recite it together each morning as you start your day and again at the end of the day when you celebrate what you've accomplished.

When the kids make strides, draw attention to how their choices have brought the vision to reality. Bring students back to the vision again when they get discouraged and off-task. Use it to help them (and you!) remember: *We have a bigger purpose here than just this one frustrating moment. We've doing big things together. We can't give up.*

Believe deeply that you are making a difference, even when you can't see it

It surprises many people to hear that I was a horrible student as a child. I never paid attention in class, talked all the time, had indecipherable handwriting, and took the easy way out for pretty much every task. By the time I got to high school, I was completely boy crazy and had zero interest in anything academic. I was lazy, disorganized, and unmotivated.

I'm sure I drove my teachers nuts. Some of them were patient with me, and others seemed to give up immediately after meeting me and figuring out "my type." I'm sure none of them imagined that one day, I'd be an entrepreneur running my own educational consulting business and publishing company (*Angela?! Angela giving advice on how to be organized and stay motivated?!*). That would probably give them a pretty good laugh!

I am grateful to those teachers who kept trying to engage me, and grateful to my parents who never gave up. They realized there's no such thing as a hopeless case, and that children are always capable of change and improvement.

There is very little immediate gratification in our work, and we have to learn to live with that. Teaching is very much like the sowing of seeds...it takes months or even years to see the fruit of our labor at times. Often the payoff from our efforts won't be evident until long after a student has left our classrooms.

Trust that your hard work will manifest in positive ways for a very long time to come. Stay focused on your vision. When you teach, you don't always get a short term reward, but you do leave a legacy. You have a choice about what that legacy will be.

10

Uncover the compelling reason for every lesson you teach

It's a question that superintendents and administrators need to ask. Teachers need to ask it, too. And just as critically, students need to ask it.

Why? Why are we doing this? Why does this matter? Why is this important?

Why is a much harder question than *how*. Teachers are rarely asked by others why we make instructional choices in the classroom, and we rarely have time to ask ourselves. Even more unfortunately, the answers we do have regarding "why" are probably not very motivating.

Why am I teaching this? Because it's on the test.

Why is it on the test? Because it's in the curriculum.

Why is it in the curriculum? Because it's in the standards.

Why is it in the standards? Because some committee somewhere decided kids should know it.

Why should my students learn this standard today? Because…well…that's what the pacing guide says? They might need the information some day? I might lose my job if I don't teach it?

I spent many years of my teaching career without having any clue about how to come up with meaningful answers to those questions, and it created severe burnout.

At the time, I would have blamed it on the testing, the lack of freedom to teach, or having too many kids in my classroom. But the real reason I was burning out was because I felt like a cog in a broken system. I felt like most of the things I was forced to do in the classroom did not benefit my kids, and therefore, my work did not matter.

What's the purpose of having kids learn this, anyway?

I often wondered, *How am I supposed to inspire my students and help them tap into their inner motivation when half of my curriculum has no relevance to kids' lives? How am I supposed to be passionate about teaching when most of what I do is test prep? What do I do with those skills and topics that I can't even bring* myself *to care about, much less get my kids to care about?*

Here's an example of what I was struggling with. My standards required me to teach students how to find the area of an irregular shape using the strategy of counting up squares on grid paper. And so I taught it, year after year. I gave these bi-weekly multiple choice benchmark assessments in which the kids had to count 42 little squares and half squares, and it took them forever and they kept losing their place and I had to mark their answers wrong because they were off by one square even though they clearly knew the process and I tested them on it again and again and again…and *for what*, exactly?

Sure, learning about the area of irregular spaces helped prepare them for higher level math classes, but what's the purpose of including it in middle and high school?

Do we teach it because there's a small chance a kid might become an architect or enter some other field in which people calculate the area of irregular spaces in their everyday work?

Or maybe because they might want to put carpet in an irregularly shaped room in their house one day? And in this crazy version of the future, the internet doesn't exist, there's no such thing as a professional carpet installer, and the kids are certain to remember a math skill they learned 20 years ago and haven't used since?

The real truth that none of us want to admit is this: *we often don't see a good reason for kids to learn the things we're tasked with teaching them.* No wonder we feel like it's so hard to get kids to buy into a lesson—we don't believe in the importance of it ourselves!

2 ways NOT to get kids invested in boring, irrelevant material

When the alleged real life purpose for a concept is not that meaningful, we tend to do one of two things. Sometimes we plow forward with the dry material and force it on our students. We ignore the fact that no one is truly invested in the topic, and when the kids start dozing off, we plead with them: "Hey guys, I know this is kinda boring. Let's just get it over with and then we can do something more fun."

The other thing we sometimes try is dressing up the concept a bit to make it more "authentic." You know how this goes—we create word problems like, *What is the square footage of Miley Cyrus' stage which just so happens to be irregularly-shaped?*

Placing unmeaningful skills in a slightly more relevant context does work, but only part of the time. That's because not all kids care about Miley Cyrus, and even fewer of them care enough about her to put in the hard work needed to determine the size of her stage. Placing a problem in an artificial context for kids doesn't necessarily mean the kids are going to think the work is relevant and important. Sometimes that approach leads to *more* student disengagement: the kids who hate Miley Cyrus now have even less incentive to work.

And so we get stuck in this horrible pattern of launching into instruction on concept after concept without really knowing how or why it's going to benefit students. We're grasping for real-world connections and seeking to entertain our students instead of engage them. We make the mistake of believing that learning must be fun when in fact real learning is often hard work. Real learning is centered around engagement and meaning, and struggle for mastery is often the very thing that makes it enjoyable.

How does this benefit my students right now?

Without our *own* compelling reason for teaching a lesson, it's really difficult to get *kids* invested in their learning. So it's very important to start your lesson planning by answering the "why."

Once you know the compelling reason and deeper purpose for a concept, you will immediately become more excited about teaching it. Your passion and clarity of focus will become contagious and draw kids into the topic.

The importance of a learning task does not necessarily stem from the possibility of a student becoming an architect or fiction writer or physicist one day. The task must, in some way, benefit them right now. Will the task help them become better critical thinkers or cooperative learners? Will it help them become more disciplined in their work habits? Will it give them a new strategy for problem solving? Will it help them apply their skills to a new context, or sharpen and refine skills they've already learned?

Figure out what students will gain from completing the task and stay focused on that as you plan and teach. Then share with students the benefit you've uncovered.

When we truly believe in the purpose of an activity, we enjoy teaching more and do it with greater effectiveness. And when students truly believe in the purpose—when they discover the personal advantage and consider their unique, individual reasons for learning—real engagement happens.

Let students uncover the WHY

We can't forget that part of our job is to help students figure out why they need to learn a particular skill and how it will benefit them personally. This doesn't have to be a complicated process—just ask "why" at the beginning of your lesson and let the kids brainstorm.

When you first try this, you'll probably get the same outcome that I did with my students—most of them really don't know how to figure out the why, especially if it's not obvious. So, they'll mostly talk about potential benefits in the future: *It will help me get to the next grade; it could help me in my job one day; it will help me pass the test.*

If your students give answers like that, it's okay. Just keep bringing them back to the present moment. Most kids will not be motivated to persevere through difficult work just by the possibility of getting an A on their report card, much less a goal even further in the future like passing the grade level or getting a good job. So, help kids stay focused on the benefits they will enjoy *now*.

Sometimes it's easier for kids to grasp the "why" once the lesson has already started. Use a good hook or anticipatory set to draw them in, and once they start learning, help kids make connections between that day's lesson and the skills they learned previously.

After the lesson, encourage students to reflect on how they've benefited from putting forth the effort to learn: "Why did we learn this? How are you more skilled at ___ now than you were an hour ago?"

When students know you're going to ask, "Why did we learn this?" after a lesson, they will automatically start thinking about the "why" upfront and look for compelling reasons to learn all throughout the lesson.

Thinking about the "why" after a lesson helps students see that learning doesn't just happen in big light bulb moments. Most benefits come through slow, steady, repeated practice. If you teach kids to look for that, they'll notice those small wins and will be more motivated to put in the hard work needed to be successful.

Don't just post objectives—post questions, too!

Most teachers are required to post learning targets, objectives, and standards for every lesson we teach. We spend massive amounts of time copying and displaying the information to please administrators, grumbling at how it's a waste of time because the students never read or refer to it.

I absolutely love this quote from Krissy Venosdale: "Posting a lesson target before teaching a lesson is like announcing what a gift is before it's opened. Post a question. Bring curiosity and thinking back to the classroom!"

Why not start your lesson with a really compelling question for kids to answer? Use essential questions to drive your instruction and help kids uncover a greater purpose for what they're learning. Invite students to submit their own questions, too, so they can move beyond the objectives posted and answer a question they truly care about.

Some of the best student engagement I've ever seen has come through project-based learning. If you really want to see kids who are passionate about what they're doing in the classroom, give them the opportunity to explore an authentic question that they care about through a project they have some say in creating.

Make the learning matter in the real world

Kids need to have a meaningful purpose for their work, just like we as teachers do. They need to believe that the work they're doing not only benefits them, but also has an impact on other people. Why write when no one will read it? Why problem solve when the answer doesn't matter to anyone in real life?

We need to make sure that students' learning results in changing outcomes. Students need to believe that the tasks they do make a difference beyond the four walls of the classroom. Student engagement comes naturally when kids identify a need or problem in the world and create ways to use the skills you've taught them to meet those needs and solve those problems.

My friend Jenny teaches 3rd grade and blogs about it at Luckey Frog's Lily Pad. Last spring, her class completed an amazing project that I think is the perfect example of making learning matter in the real world. Since the class had already finished their standardized testing for the year and Jenny had a little bit more flexibility in the curriculum and scheduling, she helped the kids design a cross-curricular project which made a big impact.

Her students identified a need in their community: they wanted to help people in a nearby town who were affected by tornados. One of the kids got the idea to sell lemonade. Here are just a few of the skills her kids practiced: they estimated their costs, raised capital, asked the PTA to become an investor, created a Google form to organize parent volunteers and a doc to create a schedule, made persuasive advertisements, did a science experiment to find the best lemonade recipe, counted the money they made, and wrote thank you notes.

Her students' learning resulted in *changing outcomes*: their hard work wasn't just to get an A on a paper—their work mattered to other people. It had a positive impact on the victims of the tornado.

Though it probably won't be possible to do something like that for every lesson you teach, I encourage you to use stories like this as an inspiration, and make your students' learning matter in the real world in any way you can.

Give students an authentic audience for their work

It's been said that if your students are sharing their work with the world, they want it to be *good*. If they're just sharing it with you, they want it to be good enough.

You will see your students really come alive in the classroom when you help them design work for a real audience. Who would be excited about writing an essay when the only person who's going to read it is the teacher (and she's just going to mark it up and explain everything that's wrong with it)?

Try to publish kids' work as much as possible, even if it's just on a school website or class blog. Students can post directly to the blog or send their posts to a designated team of students in your classroom who have permission to post. They can write about what they're learning in class, post videos of themselves talking about their opinions on various topics, and upload images of projects or other work they've completed.

Invite other students to view the work, or buddy with a teacher friend and have your classes share their accomplishments with each other. Teach kids how to comment appropriately and give feedback on each other's learning.

Incorporate life and character skills you're passionate about

Another way to uncover a compelling reason for teaching and learning is to incorporate life and character skills. These include skills like understanding media bias, evaluating whether an online source is credible, and crafting a persuasive oral argument. You can lump these into 21st century skills (which we'll examine more closely in the next chapter), but really, I'm just referring to skills and characteristics that kids need in order to be successful in *life*: things like optimism, perseverance, grit, creativity, negotiation skills, compassion, and initiative.

Make a list of the life and character skills that you are passionate about teaching to students. Think of all the qualities or traits you complain that students don't have because no one is taking time to foster them. Then consider how you can incorporate those life and character skills into the lessons which you don't otherwise have a compelling reason for teaching.

Let's say you're planning a unit on erosion: you don't care much about soil and your kids care even less. What *are* you excited to teach? Look at the list of topics you're passionate about and those real life and character lessons or 21st century skills you enjoy teaching. Maybe you're passionate about conservation and teaching kids to care for our planet. So, tie in a lesson on beach erosion, and have kids figure out a way they can save a local beach.

Or let's say you're not passionate about grammar. Are you passionate about helping kids develop persuasive speaking skills and learn to confidently share their ideas with others? Have kids create a pitch to explain the best way to know whether a comma belongs in a sentence or not, and try to persuade their classmates to use that strategy when editing. If you're passionate about using technology to improve learning, have kids find 3 good apps for practicing grammar, create a rubric for evaluating them, and then select a winning app and use it to teach another class of students those skills.

Life and character skills are the things that really matter and that make teachers' work so, so important. Kids generally don't learn life and character skills from activities in the teachers' manual and multiple choice tests. These are skills that require a caring teacher to personalize the learning and make it matter on a deep level. You have the opportunity to do that every day in your classroom and I promise, it will be absolutely transformational in your sense of passion for your work as well as students' engagement.

We are ALL learners here

Sometimes a lesson is not very compelling for students because they sense there is one right answer to every question. Kids are acutely aware that the teacher already knows the correct response and is waiting impatiently for them to get it. They see other students arriving at the answer more quickly and get frustrated. Then they give up and plead, "Why can't you just *tellll meeeee* the answer?"

It's far more motivating to learn something *with* someone else and discover the answer together. So, join in on the learning process! Try to ask your students questions that you don't know the answer to. Nothing makes a child feel more valued than when he or she is able to contribute something to the classroom that the teacher was genuinely not able to accomplish alone.

For many teachers, an obvious area of application for this is technology. Students often know more than we do about tech, and it's just not possible for any one person to know everything about such a fast-changing topic, anyway. Set up your own personal tech support team of students who are knowledgeable about various devices, and ask for their help when you or their classmates need troubleshooting assistance.

Of course, as teachers we should be highly knowledgeable about our subject matter and pedagogy. But we don't need to be the expert on every topic and situation that arises. Give yourself permission to learn with students. Don't worry—they won't respect you any less! You're not going to say "I don't know" and leave it at that. Instead, you'll model good problem solving strategies. Tell the class, "I'm not sure—let's Google it" and demonstrate how to use online search tools to find information.

One of the most powerful tools you have for student engagement is to admit, "I don't know the answer; let's find it together." When you're discovering the answer as a team, the question immediately takes on more significance because there's an authentic, shared purpose.

Creating a classroom environment in which you both explicitly and implicitly state that *we are ALL learners here* gives kids permission to take risks and fail...and it gives you permission, too. Learn together. Discover the "why" together. It's simpler than you think to make each lesson personally meaningful for every member of the classroom community.

11

Create curriculum "bright spots" you can't wait to teach

I'd like to tell you that the prospect of connecting with students and changing lives is enough to motivate me to climb out of that warm bed when the alarm goes off each morning. But I have to admit, that's not always the case.

I think we all have days when we're exhausted, don't feel well, or have so much else going on at school or at home that the idea of facing another long day in the classroom makes us want to stay under the covers.

One trick for increasing your daily motivation and starting the school day with energy and optimism is to intentionally create bright spots in your daily routine and curriculum.

Bright spots are little rewards and enjoyable activities that help compensate for the test prep drudgery and break up the monotony of the more mundane and difficult aspects of your work.

It's okay if you don't enjoy teaching every single standard

Are there any lessons or skills in your curriculum that you just dread teaching? If so, you're not alone! Most teachers have specific topics that we don't really enjoy teaching, as well as topics for which we don't have a lot of experience or expertise.

This issue is often more pronounced for elementary teachers who must prepare lessons for 4-7 subjects per day. There are very few of us who are truly skilled at and legitimately enjoy teaching every unit for math *and* reading *and* writing *and* science *and* social studies.

As a third grade teacher, my weakest subject was science, especially earth science. And though I felt confident in my understanding of non-science skills like subject-verb agreement and geometric lines and angles, I did not enjoy teaching them.

These were topics that I really struggled to make enjoyable for students and relevant to their lives. Much of the content was also hard to explain and the kids rarely had a true understanding of it, which only compounded the problem. I muddled through the instruction half-heartedly for many years, just trying to "get the unit over with" so we could move on to something more interesting.

If you can relate to that attitude of "just get it over with," I hope this chapter will help you approach your teaching in a new way. We have a potentially life-changing opportunity to fuel students' curiosity and potential interest in every topic we teach—why squander that by making kids sit through boring, passionless lessons? I think kids deserve to have a passionate teacher who lights a spark within them, and I think teachers deserve to have incredible lessons that we look forward to implementing.

So, resist the urge to throw all your energy into planning your favorite subjects and units. If you enjoy a subject inherently, it's not going to need as much improvement and your passion will naturally make the lesson more engaging. Instead, try to develop enjoyable lesson ideas that can serve as bright spots in units of instruction that would otherwise be hard to teach with enthusiasm.

Incorporate your favorite activities or learning strategies

One of the best ways to create bright spots is by building in more of the things you love doing with students in the classroom. Think back to your positive teaching memories—those times when lessons went really well and kids mastered the content with enthusiasm. Make a list of those favorite activities, being as specific as possible. My list includes gallery walks, student-directed projects, online games, read alouds, learning stations, and experiments.

You might want to take or find photographs of your favorite strategies and curate them via Pinterest as I've done, or find related resources online and use a bookmarking tool to keep your ideas organized in one place.

Then, refer to that list or collection of ideas when you've got a relatively uneventful week ahead or need an idea to spice up a lesson you're not crazy about. It's especially useful to incorporate ideas from the list during weeks when you're giving a lot of tests or test prep activities so that you and the kids have some fun lessons to look forward to.

I mentioned that I, personally, found our third grade earth science topics pretty boring and I wasn't very confident in my own ability to teach that subject well. But one of my favorite things to teach kids is how to make a pop-up book: it's super easy and I've yet to meet a child who isn't mesmerized by the process.

So, at the beginning of our earth science unit, I would read the class a pop-up book I created as a model. There was one page for each type of slow and fast land change, with each page featuring a pop-up picture and a paragraph description with the land change definition and at least 5 details about it.

Reading the book was a great introduction to the concepts we would be studying, and after the last page, I announced that students would be creating their own pop-up books. That got the kids excited about the unit and gave them a reason to learn, since they wouldn't be able to write an informative book if they didn't understand the content.

As we studied each topic in our earth science unit, students created a corresponding page for their pop-up books. At the end of the unit, they read one another's books to review the concepts and created their own book-based quizzes for their classmates.

Though I never became an earth science expert or enthusiast, the pop-up book activity gave me something to look forward to during that unit. I no longer had the attitude of "let's just get it over with" because I had created an ongoing related activity that was enjoyable for me to do with the kids.

Create a fun unit-long project

As you can tell from the pop-up book activity, I hate the idea of having a long, dry unit the kids and I have to suffer through before we can get to the fun culminating project at the end. Why wait to enjoy teaching and learning? I like to tie my daily instruction into an engaging project as often as possible.

Before the standards were changed a few years ago, third graders in Florida were required to memorize and distinguish between various types of lines and angles in geometry. It was an extremely frustrating unit for all of us because there were only so many real world connections I could make for 8-year-olds in regard to a line segment versus a ray. (Not to mention I had to constantly distinguish between *a ray* and *array*, which was another term they'd just learned and never seemed to encounter in the real world.)

One year, I'd had enough of the lines and angles tedium and decided to turn my students into reporters. I told them at the start of the unit that they'd be writing a news article for our website explaining the different types of angles and lines, and where each could be found in our community. I chose to have students post these articles to our existing class blog to keep things simple, but I could have taken the idea even further, starting a new blog just for this project and calling it "The Geometry Times" or some title the kids selected.

I purchased mini spiral notepads (6 for $1) and gave one to each student. Older students who can type more adeptly would probably prefer doing the note-taking on a computer or tablet, but notepads worked best for my class.

As I instructed the kids on various geometry terms, they took notes in their mini notepads. They created one page for each line or angle, defined it, drew it, and jotted down some examples we discussed. This gave them a break from writing in their math journals and played into the newspaper reporter angle.

The kids then worked in groups to write their articles, incorporating photographs of different angles and lines they'd found around the school and community. After a thorough peer editing process, they published their articles on the blog for other classes and their family members to read and comment on.

I could have just had the kids take regular notes in their math journals and participate in a real life lines/angles hunt with a summary blog post at the end of the unit. That's not a bad approach to use.

But the simple gimmick of students being reporters who had to take notes for their news article got the kids excited to learn about obtuse and acute angles *every day* leading up to the fun culmination. Taking notes can be boring, but they loved whipping out their special mini notepads and jotting down important facts for their stories…and their enthusiasm got me more excited about teaching geometry.

Use student-directed workstations

Sometimes you may not need to give much direct instruction on a topic at all, and can instead allow students to direct the learning and explore the concept at their own pace.

For example, I had to spend a few school years teaching students some subject-verb agreement concepts that made me want to pull my hair out. Eventually, I tried having students explore the topic with partners in workstations.

There was a station in which students intentionally wrote incorrect sentences and switched papers with a partner to correct; an iPod station where they listened to an audio recording of me reading a passage with incorrect grammar and were tasked with recording themselves reading it correctly; and a station where they read a short story, identified the subject and the verb in any 5 sentences from the story, and then re-wrote the sentences using a different conjugation.

Each day for three days, I conducted a 5 minute mini-lesson with the class and then gave the kids 10 minutes to work in one of the stations, so that by the end of the three days, every student had completed all three stations. The kids loved it and retained the information so much better than in the past where my lesson consisted of guiding them through the completion of grammar worksheets.

It took me about a half an hour to plan and create the workstations (as opposed to two minutes for running off copies of the worksheets), but I never again dreaded teaching subject-verb agreement to students, so it was time well spent!

Make boring concepts more rigorous by incorporating 21st century skills

The term "21st century skills" simply refers to modern ways of thinking and working that students will need in order to be successful in various aspects of life. The Partnership for 21st Century Skills identifies three different types of these skills that you can integrate in your regular curriculum. Doing so is a terrific way to bring boring, rote learning up to date.

The first type is Life and Career Skills. As you're teaching, help kids identify how they can use the information in their future careers. Have them role play, interview someone in the field, or research ways the skills are used by people in their jobs. You can also help students make connections between the content and their personal lives: how is the lesson going to help them manage a personal budget, choose which car to buy, predict the weather, determine the best route to a destination, or make healthy meals?

Another type of 21st century skills is Information, Media, and Technology Skills. Expose students to different types of media and information online and help them think critically about it: Is the information accurate? How do they know? Give kids the opportunity to practice technology skills, too—that's a fantastic way to make content more engaging, challenging, and differentiated.

It doesn't have to be complicated—you can start by choosing just one or two open-ended web tools or apps that can be used for a variety of concepts, and experiment with different uses in the classroom throughout the year. For example, students can use the free app Show Me to explain their strategies in math, summarize a process in science, describe a historical event in social studies, and retell a story in language arts. You can slowly add in more apps and web tools as the year progresses, and give students choice over how they want to practice information literacy skills and demonstrate what they've learned.

The third type of 21st century skills is my favorite: Learning and Innovation Skills, also known as the 4 Cs. They are: critical thinking, communication, collaboration, and creativity. Why not have kids collaborate and think critically while learning potentially dry topics like historical dates or scientific formulas? Use partner and group work activities throughout the day, and provide opportunities for kids to create rather than just consume content. That will automatically add a level of rigor that makes the task more engaging for kids, and will bring new excitement to otherwise boring lessons.

The more you integrate 21st century skills like these into your teaching, the more natural it will feel. Start slowly—perhaps with the topics you're most comfortable with, and then add them throughout your curriculum. As you infuse 21st century skills into dated, rote, or boring standards, you'll start to see the curriculum come alive…and that will make you and the kids come alive, too.

Spend one hour a month looking for engaging ways to teach a topic you dread

You might be thinking, *All of these ideas sound great, but how do I come up with them?* Contrary to popular belief, thinking up engaging teaching strategies doesn't require you to be a particularly creative person. It's simply a matter of immersing yourself in great resources and giving yourself time to explore and consider them. When you focus on one very specific standard or skill, I think you'll be amazed at the quality of ideas you'll come up with.

Here's a really efficient way to do that. As you plan for your upcoming units of study, reflect on whether there are any concepts, skills, or lessons that you wish you could skip because they're either boring or extremely difficult for students to master. Then spend just one hour online looking for ways to make the lessons more interesting and meaningful for students.

You can start with a Google search: type in a query such as *activities for teaching* ___, *lesson ideas for* ___, or ___ *activities for kids*. If you get too many results or they're not what you're looking for, add your grade level to the search, i.e. *lesson ideas for American Revolution 7th grade*. You can also do a Google image search and view those results instead: you'll find pictures of centers, games, and other activities, and can click the pictures to learn more about them.

In your search results, look for links to teacher message board forums, as those are likely to have conversations between teachers about different ways they teach the topic. Blog post articles are another good find in many instances—don't forget to scroll down to the comments to see what ideas were shared there, too.

You can also run a search on Pinterest. I tend to get good results from typing in the grade level followed by the topic, such as *5th grade rounding decimals*. You generally won't get as many results through Pinterest as you will through Google, but sometimes searching the entire internet can be a little overwhelming. Pinterest simplifies the process a bit and makes it more visual.

Another good way to find interesting ideas is to ask other teachers online. Post your dilemma to a teachers' Facebook group or on Twitter and see what other people suggest. If you want to simplify the process, you can go to sites like TeachersPayTeachers.com to find ready-to-go lesson resources that have been developed and tested by other educators.

You can certainly spend longer than an hour looking for new ideas, but setting that time limit makes the task seem less daunting and also prevents you from getting sucked into an internet black hole. I've found that just 30 minutes is usually more than enough time to find an idea for an anchor chart, a song/video, and a hands-on activity. Discovering a new lesson you're excited to try will make tackling that topic you formerly dreaded something you can actually look forward to.

Create daily bright spots in your schedule

In addition to planning bright spots in dull curriculum, I also found it helpful to build at least one little bright spot into my daily schedule for each day of the week. I've always planned fun activities for students and sprinkled them throughout our routines—that's a habit that is ingrained in us as teachers. But it took me many years to realize that I, too, needed fun things to look forward to and little rewards for a job well done, and that I couldn't afford to wait for someone else to meet that need.

One year, I had a particularly challenging class and regularly woke up in the middle of the night with a knot in my stomach. There were many days when I wished I was anywhere but in my classroom, and trying to hide that from the kids was sucking the life out of me. I really, really needed something to look forward to each day that would motivate me to give 100%.

Here are some of the bright spots I planned for that year:

Mondays: This was the hardest day of the week for me, so a co-worker and I took turns bringing breakfast to school before our workday hours officially started. We ate together in her classroom and chatted about the previous weekend. It was such a nice way to ease into the workweek.

Tuesdays: I'd enrolled my students in a virtual class that was taught by the school district remotely, giving me a little bit of a break for 30 minutes on Tuesday mornings. While my students were watching the teacher's lesson on the interactive whiteboard screen, I could usually prepare the materials I needed for the rest of the week's lessons, which left me feeling energized instead of constantly behind.

Wednesdays: I team-taught a reading lesson with an enthusiastic co-worker who always got me excited about our work. It was fun to teach students other than my own for awhile, and it was also enjoyable to have another adult in the room to share my day with. She gave me excellent insight into my students' learning processes and also commiserated with me on some of the problems I was facing. Team teaching made me feel a bit less isolated in my classroom.

Thursdays: I invited students who had met certain goals for the week to eat lunch with me in the classroom. We'd watch a Magic School Bus episode together or just sit and chat. The students often behaved much differently when they were apart from the rest of the class, and I was able to behave differently, too, because I wasn't tasked with making sure they were doing their work or achieving a learning outcome. I was able to connect with them as individuals, and that was amazingly energizing.

Fridays: The kids who had completed their work for the week got extra center time while the rest of the group caught up on their assignments. This was a 20 minute period in which students were engaged in meaningful learning in self-selected centers, but I was not responsible for teaching. I could either catch up on my own tasks, or work with the kids in a relaxed, informal way. For most students, this was the highlight of their week, and I enjoyed participating in something that they loved so much.

Think broadly about the daily bright spots that could work for *your* schedule. Maybe there's a student who always makes you laugh and you look forward to calling on him or her because you never know what's going to be said. Or maybe there's a fun colleague you'll get to collaborate with in a meeting. Your bright spot could also be a daily routine you particularly enjoy or a long-term professional project you try to work on regularly.

Whenever you start to feel dread about going to school, remind yourself of the bright spots you have planned and stay focused on them instead of whatever is stressing you out. As you wake up each morning, train yourself not to think about yesterday's mistakes or all the things that could go wrong today, but about those bright spots: the child who beams at you when he enters the classroom; the colleague whose humor at lunchtime puts everything in perspective; that cool new teaching idea you're excited to experiment with.

Don't wait for something enjoyable to happen: plan for it! Be intentional. Create bright spots not only for your students, but also for yourself.

12

Incorporate playfulness and have fun with learning

For many of you, being playful with students and having fun in the classroom is a no-brainer. It's an approach that you follow intuitively, and being a little bit crazy with your kids to amuse them (and yourself) is something you can't imagine not doing. You're always on the lookout for new and creative ideas, and this chapter won't disappoint!

But playfulness in the classroom isn't something that comes naturally to everyone. It certainly doesn't for me.

I'm friendly and warm when I teach, but learning is serious business to me. I don't like to get kids all riled up and then have to calm them down. It's my tendency to stay focused on the task at hand and keep the kids focused, too. I've got a specific goal I'm trying to accomplish by the end of the lesson, and I don't particularly enjoy anything that distracts from that goal.

Several years ago, I decided to make a conscious effort to be more playful in the classroom. Here's how—and why—I did it.

Create emotional experiences that make content memorable

When I took a class on effective teaching methods for my master's degree, I read a lot of research regarding the connection between emotions and learning. I learned that we as humans remember things which provoke an emotional reaction in us: movies that made us cry, books that made us laugh, and conversations that got us angry. Things don't often "stick" in our minds long-term unless we have some connection to them, and generating emotions is a highly effective way to create that connection.

I realized that by being so serious and focused in the classroom, I was actually making it harder for my students to remember the content! I was not creating enough *experiences* for kids. I was not providing learning opportunities that tapped into their emotions and made them *feel something*...and if you don't feel something, you're not as likely to remember it.

I started creating more experiences that created strong emotions in kids. In social studies, we'd do activities that allowed students to experience the indignation of being treated unfairly due to feudalism in medieval Europe. In science, I showed video clips of communities that had been devastated by natural disasters and animal species that had nearly reached extinction to foster a deep sense of empathy. When teaching kids how to write a strong persuasive essay, I shared editorials that created outrage or excitement and moved the kids to action.

Playful learning makes teaching more fun

Perhaps most importantly, I started looking for ways to foster more humor and laughter in the classroom. Happiness is a powerful emotion and we tend to remember moments of joy very well. Plus, kids learn better when they're in a good mood. So why not do everything possible to support them in that?

I started to experiment with...shall we say...*controlled* play and humor in the classroom. When I taught PreK, music and dance held a fundamental role in our day, but I'd been scared to try it out with older kids and risk looking like an idiot. Slowly, I incorporated activities like singing songs, transforming myself into various characters, and turning more of our tasks into games.

I wasn't surprised that the kids loved it...but I was shocked to realize how much more *I enjoyed the kids* when I was playful with them.

I had to fight the temptation to just push through lessons and *get to the point*, and sometimes the moments of silliness felt extraneous to me. But I loved looking around the room at those smiling faces and seeing my students have fun. How can you not smile when you hear a room full of giggles? Those moments of playfulness were a reminder that my students were *people*, with the same feelings and needs I have, and not little automatons that I could just program information into.

I was also surprised to see how far a little playfulness went in terms of student engagement. I could just read off the words on a vocabulary list and get half the class to follow along, or I could use an accent or silly voice and have every student at rapt attention! Though it appears that being playful with learning takes more effort, you actually conserve a lot of energy in not constantly trying to get kids' attention and force them to participate.

Even if it goes against your instincts to be a little silly in the classroom, I hope you'll experiment with some of the ideas in this chapter. Try choosing one that fits your personality, and let it evolve from there. I truly believe that integrating play in the classroom will create a more inviting place to learn, make your lessons more memorable, build a rapport with kids, *and* make teaching more enjoyable.

Integrate music in creative ways

Music is one of the most powerful tools you have to get kids' attention and tap into their emotions. Invite your students to help you create a class playlist. Make sure they understand the criteria for school-appropriate music, and allow them to suggest songs to play in class.

You can also challenge students to think of a theme song that somehow ties into each unit of study. The connection might be tenuous, at best, but it's a great way to get kids thinking deeply about what they know, and every time they hear the song, they'll think of your lessons! Play the theme song at the beginning of the class period during your warm-up, in the middle as a dance break, or at the end to celebrate learning.

During your instruction, incorporate song lyrics whenever you can. If you're one of those people who have a song pop until their heads all the time like me, share it with the kids! It doesn't matter if you sing it or say it—the lyrics will wake kids up and get them tuned in to the lesson.

Use songs to help transition between lessons and activities, too. The song could have lyrics about cleaning up or the task at hand, but it doesn't have to. You could allow the kids to vote on one popular song each month to be your designated transition song, and whenever they hear it come on, they'll know it's time to transition to the next activity.

Play the beginning of the song at a very low volume for a 30 second warning, and then turn it up louder when you want kids to start cleaning up. Teach students that the goal is for them to have all materials put away and be sitting in their seats ready for the next activity by the time the song ends. Once they've practiced this, you won't have to say, "10 more seconds!" or "Come on, you should be cleaning up!" Just turn the song on and let it do the work for you.

Even if you're not confident in your singing abilities, try singing directions (or even part of your lesson) to students. The sound is guaranteed to rise above the noise of any side conversations, and it's also a great technique when you're tired repeating yourself. If you feel like yelling because no one is listening to you, burst into song instead. You can even turn it into a joke—"You guys know how terrible my singing is. If you don't follow my directions the first time, I'm going to have to sing them. Loudly."

Have a 30 second dance break

A friend of mine received one of those talking cookie jars as a gag gift. The jar plays James Brown's song "I Feel Good." She decided that the opening activity for her first graders' morning meeting would be to open that cookie jar and dance together. It took less than a minute out of her instructional time and got all the kids alert and ready to learn. She also noticed the number of tardies declined because the kids didn't want to get to school late and miss the dance party. I think this is a fabulous idea for after lunch, as well, to wake the kids out of the afternoon slump.

This type of 30 second dance break is also a great way to celebrate students' hard work. When kids make a major breakthrough in their learning or finish a particularly intense task, say, "You all worked so hard on that. I think we should celebrate with a dance party!" Play a song from a carefully selected playlist you've created, or play the song's video on YouTube (without showing the video to kids.)

Teach kids that when you turn the song off at the 30 second mark, they should strike a pose. This ends the experience on a high note rather than having all the kids whine, "Awww! Can't we do just a little more?" Give them a few seconds to look around and laugh at each other's poses, and then you can burst into applause, which is the kids' signal to clap also and take their seats again. Do a few practice rounds of these expectations so the kids get good at it, and then you can feel confident about doing the dance party at any time without it becoming unmanageable.

If you're worried that a dance party could make the kids too rambunctious, try a Freeze Dance. Randomly stop the music once or twice and require kids to freeze in whatever position they're in. Teach kids that anyone who talks or doesn't freeze is out of the game.

Talk and read in various accents and voices

Have you ever gotten to the point where you talk so much, you're tired of hearing your own voice? Have your students gotten so tired of hearing one another answer questions and read aloud that they've started tuning each other out?

Changing up your voices is a really fun way to break out of the same boring routines. Give directions in a funny voice to make sure kids are listening. When you find yourself nagging at kids and creating a critical atmosphere, give your reminders in a sing-song voice or character voice instead.

Let the kids in on the fun, too. Have students read text or directions in unison using a special voice. Or, challenge them to figure out the main idea or most important fact from a lesson and share it using any voice they choose.

You can also make it a reward: once a certain behavioral or academic goal is reached, students can talk in accents for the rest of the day. I know several middle school teachers who swear this incentive is the most effective one they use!

Transform yourself into a different character

If you haven't tried this, I promise you will be amazed at how students at *all* grade levels respond. You can keep it simple and impromptu if you'd like. You might want to review the day's tasks in the accent and body language of a celebrity the kids love (or hate). Give your spelling test in the voice and mannerisms of a granny or grandpa, and add a cane, hat, and glasses if you really want to go over the top.

Or, create characters for different topics you teach and have them "visit" to facilitate a lesson. When reviewing grammar, put on a cape and transform yourself into Grammar Girl or Grammar Guy, a superhero who's there to save student writing from incomprehensibility. During a math lesson, put on a crown and become King or Queen Conversion, who bestows upon the townspeople a knowledge of how to convert fractions to decimals or quarts to gallons.

You can come up with a character idea for just about any lesson you teach! Just spend a few minutes brainstorming the possibilities, or better yet, brainstorm with a colleague. You can even get the kids involved. Tell them, "Tomorrow, we'll be learning about rainforest habitats. I wonder what 'visitor' will grace us with their presence…" Listen as the kids call out ideas, then surprise them by choosing one of the characters to dress up as the following day.

Use puppets to teach a lesson

When I was five years old, I had large puppet I called Mac the Monkey. He had long arms and legs which I could wrap around me and attach with Velcro, giving him the appearance of sitting on my hip. Miraculously, Mac survived in a box tucked away in my parent's garage, so a few years ago, I brought him into my classroom.

Since my students were immediately engaged whenever I brought Mac out, I used him whenever I taught a particularly difficult concept. Mac would teach the majority of the lesson, imparting the most important points because I knew the kids were hanging on his every word. My role was to ask him questions and let him know when the kids had questions ("Mac, what are we supposed to do after we make our inference? Oh, Mac, look, some of the boys and girls have their hands up, do you want to know what they're asking?")

I also had a small regular puppet called Spot the Dog. Spot was my silly sidekick I'd use for boring topics and when reviewing something tricky for the millionth time. I'd teach, and he'd get everything wrong. He'd say, "So, you're telling me that when I add 3 digit numbers, I start with the hundreds place..." and all the kids would groan and say, "Noooo, Spot! Start with the *ones* place!"

The possibility for puppets is almost endless. You could buy a small kit with 3-5 characters and assign them each a personality. Occasionally, you could even have a puppet on each hand and have them talk to each other and teach the entire lesson.

I've seen puppets used effectively even at the secondary level (think ventriloquist acts in which the puppet is a snarky sidekick, mumbling sarcastic jokes that the puppeteer doesn't catch.)

Just make sure you don't overuse them—a few times a month is plenty so that the puppets are viewed as a novelty and not a crutch.

Find fun props to use during routine activities

In the party supply section of a dollar store, I discovered little plastic hands on a stick that were designed to make a clapping sound if you shook the stick back and forth. I passed these out to students when they were presenting to the class or sharing a lot of ideas aloud. Though the kids normally got tired of listening and clapping for each person who talked, using the clappers made it much more exciting.

You can also hand out a makeshift or real microphone for students to speak into when sharing their answers. Another idea is to have a special "sharing chair" that is draped with decorations, and have students sit there when reading their work aloud. I've also seen teachers who provide a special hat or sash for students to wear when presenting.

I like to incorporate fun props when students are reviewing or checking their work. Kids can wear a special editor hat, badge, or button when in editing mode. Or, let students use a special pen, marker, or highlighter that's reserved just for the task of grading their papers.

Turn the task into a game

Find a weird or funny fact related to one of your lessons. Post it on the board when students first enter the room, or share it with students during morning meeting to see if they can figure out what you'll be teaching about that day. The person who guesses correctly gets to be a helper during the lesson, the team leader for a group activity, or the first to take a turn participating.

Timers are probably the easiest way to make any task into a game. Give the directions for the task, and display a timer on your interactive whiteboard so kids can see the countdown. They can race against their own personal best time, against other teams, or race to see if the entire class can be successful in the allotted minutes.

You can also make a lesson into a game show. Instead of just calling on students to provide answers to reading comprehension questions, say, "Who's ready to play 'Guess That Character'? Next contestant, come on down, and tell us which character you think might agree with this statement and point of view."

When calling on various students to answer questions, keep the rest of the class engaged by finding funny ways for them to verify if the response is accurate. If you call on a student to give an answer and it's correct, have the rest of the class say *yeeeeeee-haw, holy moly,* or *yeahhhh buddy*. You can also have them say a made-up word, like *fantabulous*! The kids will love that you're not afraid to be silly, and they'll pay better attention so they don't miss the antics.

Create a learning environment where humor is celebrated

Tell students outright that humor and silliness are always welcome unless you specifically say, "Let's get serious." Make light of problems instead of complaining about them or getting upset, and show students how to find the humor in life's inconveniences.

Encourage kids to find their own unique brand of humor. You can even designate a student volunteer as "Jokester," and have that student be responsible for having a joke any time the class needs a quick laugh.

A passionate teacher with a great sense of humor truly makes learning fun. The more you care about the curriculum and give yourself and the kids permission to laugh, the easier it will be to find the fun in teaching. Your classroom can be a place full of rigor AND students can laugh the entire day. Playfulness is often a mark of serious learning!

13

Build in periods of rest and downtime throughout your day

Todd Whittaker once said, "The best part of teaching is that it matters. The hardest part of teaching is that every moment of every day matters."

Isn't that the truth? There's just no natural downtime in teaching. There are no lessons in which it doesn't matter if the kids really "get it", or any interactions in which your words don't impact your students.

Talk about pressure!

Yet it's impossible to give 100% of yourself to your students throughout the day when you're physically exhausted and mentally drained...and you probably *will* feel that way if there's never any downtime, you're always "on", and you worry that you can't rest for even a moment.

For some reason, this whole topic is very hush-hush in most education circles. We're not supposed to admit that circulating around the classroom for seven hours a day is just too much to ask of our bodies. We can't confess that engaging in meaningful conversations with students for hours on end is overly taxing on our minds (not to mention our vocal chords.)

But I'll be very transparent in this chapter. I'm going to admit that I actively build periods of rest into my daily schedule...and if your body and mind are begging for a break, I recommend that you do the same.

How much energy expenditure is sustainable for you?

Don't hold onto some unrealistic ideal of how you think you "should" be able to perform. Don't expect yourself to have the same energy level you had earlier in your career before you had your own children and became infinitely busier. And definitely don't compare yourself to anyone else, especially a teacher who's fresh out of college and full of boundless energy or a firecracker veteran that still dresses in a different costume each day and takes her students on elaborate thematic learning adventures for each topic they study.

You're only going to feel frustrated and disappointed if you constantly worry that you're not doing as much as you should. Think about what is sustainable for *you*, keeping in mind that teaching is a marathon, not a sprint.

You can't give it all you've got for a short period of time and go home. Students are just as needy, if not more so, at 2 pm as they are at 8 am. It's confusing for them when a teacher is a bundle of energy at one moment and then slumped over at his desk passing out busy work the next.

Sustainability is key, so always view your choices within the framework of what you can maintain over the long haul. How are your instructional practices right now going to affect your energy level later in the day? The week? The year? 5 years from now?

Remember: energy, not time, is your most precious resource. As long as you're alive, you will automatically be given more time.

Your supply of energy, on the other hand, is not replenished unless you choose to conserve it and participate in activities that give you more of it.

Some of the brightest stars in education burn out after only a few years in the classroom because they try to do too much at one time, and allow the profession to become all-consuming. Take steps now to ensure that doesn't happen to you.

Sitting down for 10 minutes does not make you a bad teacher

Can I just reassure you of that right now? From student teaching onward, educators have it drilled into our brains that nothing says "lazy and uninvolved" like sitting at your desk when students are in the room. Being caught doing this can be the kiss of death if you happen to have a surprise administrator walk-through or observation.

The origin of the no-sitting principle is correct: generally, it's not a good thing for teachers to sit down too often. The kids start to goof off (proximity control is one of your best classroom management tools) and it's harder to be actively involved with the learning process when you're sitting. This is true.

But let's keep it real here. I, personally, cannot be on my feet teaching from 8:00 am to 2:30 pm (or longer) five days a week, especially on an unforgiving concrete floor. I've tried it, and it's exhausting even as a young and healthy person. There are times when I simply have to get stuff done in the classroom and my back, legs, and feet are aching. And so I *sit*.

3 ways to sit while teaching and still keep the kids engaged

For me, it's very important to have a place to sit down at the front of the classroom for those moments when I'm about to collapse with exhaustion. I prefer to teach when standing because that position commands more authority, but it's nice to have a seat to rest my body against on occasion.

I went to a thrift store and spent $10 on a tall stool for this very purpose. Because of the stool's height, I can see everyone in the class just as well as if I were standing, and I can be back on my feet in a split second when needed.

I was also fortunate to inherit a rocking chair from a retiring teacher. I often have students sit on the rug at my feet while I teach, providing a nice break from the regular routine for all of us. If you teach older students or kids who don't want to sit on the floor, have them pull their chairs over to your instructional area. It can be wonderful for both behavior management and student engagement to have all the kids sitting very close to you throughout the lesson.

A third way to sit is using a rolling chair. Instead of walking around to help students and bending or crouching down to assist them, stay seated and roll over to each student's work area. This is *not* a strategy you want to use all day, every day, unless you have a physical limitation. But a rolling chair can be useful for short periods of time and can even help facilitate thoughtful conversations since you're not towering over the kids.

2 ways to sit while supporting students during independent work periods

Maybe this doesn't happen at your school, but I found it wasn't unusual for the office to make an announcement that they needed some type of form sent down *immediately* even though they just mentioned it for the first time a half hour prior. Those situations leave teachers in the really tough position of having to ignore their students for 5-10 minutes (or even more) while they scramble to complete paperwork or send off an email.

The obvious solution is to have students work on something independently. But sitting at your desk in the corner of the room to work seems to send the message to kids that you're not paying attention, and therefore they think they can do whatever they want.

Try this. Set up a table somewhere in the classroom—if you lead small group instruction at a table, this area can do double duty. Place the table away from the classroom door if there's a window on the door and you're paranoid that everyone walking past will see you (*gasp!*) sitting down.

Whenever you need to get something urgent done or collect yourself for a few minutes while students are working independently or collaboratively, sit at the table. Then call a few students over to sit and do their work at the table with you. You can make this a privilege if you teach younger students, or use the technique to separate any kids who are being disruptive.

I liked to have my struggling learners sit with me at the table, as they frequently had questions and it was easier to provide support if they were close to me. If any observers walked in my classroom, I didn't feel pressure to immediately jump up from my seat, as I was legitimately working with students in a small group setting.

Another idea is to sit in an absent student's seat. This places you in the middle of the action, cutting down on behavioral problems and making it simple to lean over to assist anyone near you should the need arise.

Take the pressure off your body while standing up to teach

An anti-fatigue rug is a terrific investment for your classroom. These absorb shock when you're standing and relieve pressure on your joints. You can purchase a runner for the area by your board or wherever you stand the most. Some anti-fatigue rugs are very expensive, but I've gotten them for $20 at home improvement stores and they've worked so well that I've daydreamed about covering my entire classroom floor with them.

If you haven't already found a pair of comfortable shoes for teaching, it's time. As a beginning teacher, I wore inexpensive flat sandals a lot, and often even high heels. I didn't make the connection between my fatigue at the end of the day and my shoe choice until back and knee aches became a daily problem.

I invested in a single pair of super comfortable flat shoes that have lots of cushion, arch support, and all that other stuff it turns out my body needed, and wore those around the classroom most of the time. It made such a big difference for me that I slowly weeded out the cheap footwear in my closet and replaced them with better-constructed (and equally cute!) options that enabled me to stand and walk longer without pain.

Standing at the front of the room and teaching is also less physically draining when you aren't straining to make yourself heard. I know many teachers who have invested in a clip-on microphone, and they all swear it has made their teaching much less tiring. The increased volume helps them naturally command more authority when they speak, and they no longer have to raise their voices or repeat themselves endlessly. Their students also seem to like it, because it's easier for them to stay focused and hear what the teacher is saying.

Cut back on the lectures and teacher-directed activities

Just as most teachers can't stand up and move around the room for seven hours a day, most of us also can't hold the attention of an entire group of students for seven hours…and there's absolutely no reason to try.

From a pedagogical and neuroscientific standpoint, we know that kids can only listen for about 5-20 minutes (depending on their ages) before their brains are unable to process more information. They need breaks in instruction to reflect, talk, think, and move around. We also know that kids need to actively construct knowledge rather than be passive participants in the learning process.

Put simply, the person doing the most talking is the person doing the most learning. So if you're spending almost your entire day at the front of the classroom leading a discussion or activity, *you* are the primary beneficiary of all that effort, because you're the one doing all the work.

Using more student-directed activities will help your kids gain a deeper understanding of concepts. It will also help you conserve energy. You'll be able to give your vocal cords a rest since you'll be talking just to the students near you instead of projecting to the entire class, and you don't have to kill yourself trying to keep all 30 students interested in what you're saying.

So, find your personal balance between teacher-led activities and student-directed work so that you are not constantly instructing. Talk for 10 minutes, then give kids a collaborative task for 5 minutes. Repeat. Or, talk for 15 minutes, then give students a 30 minute project. The structure here will vary according to your grade level, subject area, and teaching style, but the goal is to place the responsibility for learning in the hands of your students as much as possible.

Don't hover over students the second you give an assignment

Once you've taught kids the procedures and routines for working, they won't need you every moment and will generally be able to get started on their own. So after you give directions, sit down on that stool you bought for the front of your classroom and take 30 seconds to regroup.

Breathe. Take a sip of water (or something caffeinated.) Ignore the kids who aren't getting to work yet: remind yourself that it's been literally 10 seconds, and resist the urge to swoop in and bark orders. Instead, give the kids a chance to self-correct. Don't get annoyed by the slow starters—think something positive and motivating, like: *My kids are totally going to get this. I love my job.*

After those 30 seconds are up, start walking around and encouraging students as they begin their work. Redirect kids as needed, and help the ones who haven't gotten started. Start asking questions and gently push their thinking.

Give yourself a moment to think and plan before transitioning to the next activity

Take a few seconds for yourself at the *end* of the lesson, too. One minute before the activity or assignment is over, use a signal to give a warning (you can announce "one minute left" or use a bell, chime, etc.) Give any individual reminders as needed, then sit back down on your stool.

Don't frantically rush around the room nagging the kids who aren't finishing up—they heard you already, and it's time for them to take personal responsibility (or not, and face the consequences.)

While you're sitting, take some deep breaths again. Observe your students. Plan what you're going to say next. Collect yourself. And then dive right back into teaching.

Utilize downtime during instruction

One of my favorite things to have kids do during lessons is write on individual dry erase boards. I demonstrate a strategy on the big board and then students try it on their own small boards. They hold up their boards for me to check their answers and I can give individual feedback by looking around the room and making eye contact with each student as I give him or her quick feedback.

If I give a multi-step or more complex problem, it's going to take even the fastest kids a minute or two to solve. Those are precious minutes. Sometimes I walk around the room, peeking over kids' shoulders to see their strategies or to probe their thinking.

But sometimes, especially if I'm tired and need to conserve my energy for the rest of the day, I use at least part of that 60 seconds to clear my head, look past my students and out the window, and mentally regroup. That leaves me with more energy to respond to students when they're done solving than if I'd hovered over them the entire time.

Alternate high-demand and low-demand activities

Here's a quick exercise for you. Make a written list of the type of assignments you give that require a lot of active teacher involvement. In other words, consider all the activities for which you'll be circling around the classroom over and over again to guide and redirect students. This could mean science experiments, technology-based assignments, small group work, and so on.

Then in a separate column, list the assignments that are less demanding and intense: warm up activities, worksheets, tests, practice tests, and maybe some partner activities or independent projects.

Now figure out how to take the activities in the two columns and alternate them.

Let's say you teach different classes of students throughout the day and need to give a test and a hands-on project to each class this week. Tomorrow, give your first period class the high-demand activity, your second period class the low-demand one, and so on throughout the day. The following day, switch. Except in extreme scheduling crunches, there's no reason to do a stressful project eight times in a row.

If you teach the same group of students all day, don't drag out nine thousand types of materials for a complex and raucous science investigation, and then launch immediately into another project that's going to result in massive clean up and your name being called by students over and over again. Do the science investigation, then have students reflect quietly in their journals, or give some other mellow assignment that gives you and your kids a chance to decompress. If you're feeling overstimulated and overwhelmed, many of your students probably are, too!

Play around with your schedule and exercise as much flexibility as you can. The idea is to create balance so that your "on" moments aren't as energy draining and you can have more of them.

Allocate the majority of your energy to what's most important

If the next hour's schedule requires you to give a vocabulary quiz and teach a lesson about context clues, but you know that physically you can't circulate around the room for both, give yourself permission to sit down during the quiz so you have the energy to get kids excited and engaged during your lesson.

If you're teaching an especially difficult concept in math and need to save up your dwindling reserve of patience, have your kids go over the warm-up activity answers with a partner instead of in a whole class, teacher-led discussion.

If the new app you introduced isn't letting your students export their work but tech problems always give you a headache, wait to check it out until the end of the period so you can be at your best during the remainder of the lesson.

Take time to think about your own limitations and plan around them. Experiment with different class time structures so that you can allow for low energy periods without sacrificing instructional quality.

Form a good game plan for low-energy days

Here's something else teachers aren't supposed to admit: *we all have times in our lives when we just aren't able to give 100% to the job.* Sometimes it's only for a day: maybe you hosted a birthday party for your son the evening before and are tired from cleaning up, or maybe you stayed late at school conducting parent conferences. Other times, low-energy periods last for weeks or even months, such as when going through a divorce or dealing with a family member's severe illness.

These circumstances are not a license to do a halfway job of teaching your students. They are an opportunity to recognize that you are not at your best, show yourself grace, and plan ahead in order to minimize the impact on your students.

On low-energy days, narrow your focus to what's truly most important and channel as much of your energy as possible into those aspects of your work. Cut out the "extras" and don't put pressure on yourself to go above and beyond in areas that don't really matter.

Permit yourself to do a little less by remembering that the situation is temporary: you *will* be able to work at the level you're accustomed to again, and in order to get to that level, you need to allow yourself a time of less pressure.

Even though you might feel like you're on your own, you can't be afraid to reach out to others for support when you need it. Ask a colleague to pick your students up from lunch for you or see if a team member can run off extra photocopies or gather lesson materials. You can return the favor when you're feeling better, so don't feel guilty about asking for help.

When other people offer to take responsibilities off your plate or ask if there's anything they can do to help, avoid the knee-jerk response to just say, "I'm fine, thanks anyway." Instead, have a prepared list of tasks that can be delegated, and tell people, "Thanks

so much for offering! I would really appreciate your help with ___."
Don't take away the joy that comes from helping others: empower
people who care about you to show you the support you need!

You can also admit to your *students* that you're not feeling your
best, and ask them directly for their support and cooperation. Most
kids are eager to help take on some of your responsibilities, and you
might even find that you were doing tasks that should have been
turned over to them a long time ago! I've also found that a handful
of kids will usually help out with reminders to the rest of the class
("Hey guys, be quiet, Mrs. Watson lost her voice and doesn't feel
good, remember? Don't make her shout!")

Above all, take care of yourself. That's not a selfish endeavor—a
healthy, happy teacher is the best gift you could ever give your
students.

Remember that students need downtime, too

As you plan ways to build periods of rest into your day, keep in
mind that students will benefit from this, as well. Think about the
kids in your class who are introverted, shy, socially awkward, just
learning the English language, dealing with attention deficit or
sensory/noise issues, or need extra time to process information. I'm
betting that's at least half your class! Those students desperately
need some downtime during the day.

I would even argue that *every* student benefits from periods of
rest. School is an intense place for most kids: they are expected to be
perfectly on-task for hours on end, mastering the expectations of
multiple teachers and learning increasingly challenging concepts in
many different subjects per day. They're dealing with a huge array
of social, emotional, and physical issues that we often know nothing
about. They have only a thirty minute break for lunch, spend half
that time waiting in line to get their food, and then spend the other

half sitting at a crowded table surrounded by hundreds of kids who are producing a noise level that rivals an aircraft at take-off. No wonder so many kids can't concentrate, act out in class, and have abnormally high or low energy levels!

Though students will rarely articulate it, they have a deep need for the classroom to be a sanctuary and place of tranquility. They, too, need a few moments in which they are not expected to perform and can just be themselves. They, too, need to feel like it's okay not to bring their "A" game every minute of the day and actually be a human being.

The ideas in this chapter (especially alternating high-energy and low-energy activities, and mixing independent work and collaborative work) will benefit your students as well as you. My class always loved when I'd leave the lights half on and play some relaxing classical music while they worked. They loved the quiet periods of silent reading. They appreciated the opportunity to think and write without anyone interrupting or hurrying at them.

Don't put pressure on yourself to be constantly stimulating kids' minds and pushing them to work harder. Often they, like us, will perform better when allowed to have a few moments to decompress, unwind, and regroup.

14

Construct a self-running classroom that frees you to teach

I had an illness during my third year of teaching that kept me out of my PreK classroom for nearly five weeks. Although I knew my substitute well and trusted her, I was still very nervous about what I'd find when I returned. Would our center materials be destroyed and pages of our books be ripped up? Would all of my carefully reinforced behavioral expectations be completely undone?

That first day back, I held my breath as the first couple of kids entered the room. Their faces lit up when they saw me. They rushed over to give hugs and exchange greetings. And then...they walked over to the bookshelf, chose a book, and sat down on the rug to read together, *exactly as I had taught them to do* for their morning work routine.

As I stood there slack-jawed, my principal walked in the room to welcome me back. And in that moment, she gave me one of the greatest professional compliments I've ever received. She said, "Angela, this is what they did every single morning while you were out. You got those routines so well ingrained in the kids that it didn't even occur to them to behave any differently. The kids are completely self-directed. *I couldn't even tell you were gone."*

It was an ego boost and an ego blow at the same time: my students didn't need *me* in order to learn. Even at four-years-old, they knew what to do, and they were able to do it.

That's the idea behind constructing a self-running classroom: your energy is no longer consumed with reminding kids of expectations, redirecting behavior, keeping track of which student went to the nurse and who went to the bathroom, and so on. When the classroom runs itself, your mental energy can go to what matters most and what brings the most job satisfaction: teaching, learning, and connecting with kids.

Create familiar, predictable routines that kids can depend on

The cornerstone of a self-running classroom is clearly defined routines that are followed in the same manner every single day, every single time.

From August through June, my third graders did the exact same thing every day when they arrived at school: they hung up their coats, unpacked their backpacks, used the bathroom/got a drink, sharpened pencils, and started on a morning work assignment. And I mean *every* morning, no matter what, 185 days a year.

It didn't matter if we were having a field trip or an assembly or a party later on. The day always started in the same predictable, familiar way so that students never had to wander around the room asking what they were supposed to be doing or trying to figure out what the plan was for the day.

Similarly, we had set routines for entering the classroom after P.E. and after lunch, for homework collection, for dismissal, and pretty much every other event that occurred on a daily basis. If our regular schedule was to be interrupted, I wrote a note in a designated place on our board called "Schedule Changes and Special Events" so students could reference it throughout the day and know exactly what to expect at what time. I reviewed the changes during our morning meeting and made sure to explain them to the kids again right before the change so they understood why there would be a one-time exception and what they would need to do differently.

Predictable routines give students confidence in how to behave and work in the classroom. They give kids many opportunities to practice meeting expectations, which means you're setting kids up to be successful. Students never have to stop concentrating on a project because they don't know where to find the materials. They don't have to be embarrassed about grabbing their coat when it's not time to go outside. They don't have to feel lost and left out because they don't know who their partner is for an activity.

Predictable routines make the classroom a familiar, comfortable place not only for kids, but for teachers, too. Routines enable you to expend far less energy telling kids how to complete basic tasks and explaining where kids should be and what they should be doing. If you'd like to learn more about the specific routines I chose and how I taught them to students, check out the Routines and Procedures section of my website.

Use predictable routines to support unpredictable instruction

All of those predictable routines could make for a pretty boring learning environment...except that they create a space for *instruction* to be unpredictable. There's a huge amount of variety in the types of activities I do with kids, and students are given lots of input as to how they choose to learn and demonstrate their learning. The routines simply serve as a framework, something that holds all of the other aspects of the classroom in place.

Here's an example. When you use manipulatives with your students, teach a specific procedure for distributing the materials, using them appropriately, and cleaning them up. Then be consistent with that routine—don't assign the job of distributing manipulatives to two class helpers and then decide to pass them out yourself sometimes, or tell a handful of kids to get up and get what they need.

You might be tempted to do that "just this time" thinking it will be quicker, but deviating from the procedure actually costs you time. It causes kids to look to *you* for direction that day and in every follow-up lesson instead of automatically following the *routine* you've taught.

Once you've established a routine like two Math Helpers being in charge of distributing and putting away manipulatives, you must stick to it. If a child didn't receive the materials she needs, she shouldn't tell you, ask her friends what to do, or go dig through the manipulatives herself. Those behaviors pull your attention away from student learning and create a distraction. Instead, she should quietly inform one of the Math Helpers, who will take care of the situation without you or anyone else in the class even knowing about it.

Preparing to work with manipulatives should be something kids can do quickly and on autopilot because it's always done the same way. They shouldn't have to waste precious brain power trying to figure out whose turn it is to unpack the base ten blocks. By October, you should be able to say, "We're using base ten blocks today; Math Helpers, please prepare them" and the manipulatives should magically appear in front of students as they're already starting to work on the first part of the math investigation.

This saves not only *students'* mental energy, but your own. Many teachers are hesitant to use hands-on materials because it's so difficult to manage student behaviors and deal with the clean up.

Imagine how much more often you'd use manipulatives if you knew students would stay on-task during the lesson and handle all the distribution and collection with only a single directive from you!

When students understand and follow predictable routines, you are free to become creative with your instruction. Your mental energy is no longer consumed with figuring out the logistics of simple tasks. You get to try different teaching strategies and experiment with all kinds of fun activities. Students' behavior and basic classroom management becomes a no-brainer so you can really innovate with students. Teaching becomes exciting again!

Use the 3 Before Me Rule to empower students to answer their own questions

In a self-running classroom, students not only know the basic routines for tasks, but they also know how to get additional information when needed. They don't depend on the teacher to repeat himself, give constant affirmations, or hand hold through procedures ("Yes, I said you can get a drink right now. Yes, you can get a book to read from right there when you're done.")

Teach students that whenever they have a procedural question, they should use the 3 Before Me Rule and ask three other students before they ask you. If you've explicitly taught kids when they can get drinks from the water fountain and what to do when they're finished with an assignment, they don't have to interrupt you if they're having trouble remembering or just want to make sure they're doing the right thing, because everyone around them knows what to do and can easily help out.

I like to teach students that the first person they should ask is themselves. Many times students blurt out questions without bothering to consider the answer because it's easier to get someone else to do the thinking for them. Teach students to have confidence in themselves and be independent thinkers—if they're not sure what to do, they should try to think of the solution first. If they're truly not sure, they should ask a friend nearby. If that person isn't sure, they can ask another friend. If the three of them don't have the answer, then it's appropriate to ask the teacher.

Anytime students try to problem solve this way and accidentally follow an incorrect procedure, give a gentle, quiet reminder. Don't make a big deal or yell about it, because that will create teacher dependence: students will want to check in with you before making any decisions so that they don't get in trouble.

It's also important to distinguish between 3 Before Me questions (which are based on routines or expectations you've already taught and therefore anyone in the class should be able to reinforce) and questions only the teacher can answer (which are related to content or personal situations.) If you model and practice this rule effectively, then the next time a student asks, "What page are we on right now?" you can simply smile and hold up 3 fingers.

Give directions that kids will follow the first time

It's important to speak up and say exactly what you need from students. There have been many times when I gave directions and heard the kids whispering to each other, "What'd she say?" even though I was certain I'd been perfectly clear. I realized that often when I gave the first part of a direction, the classroom began buzzing with the noise of students starting to get materials from their desks and whispering to each other. That caused me to assume they knew what to do, and I didn't command the same attention for the remainder of the directions. I've had to be very mindful about enunciating the full set of directions instead of just trailing off.

You might find it helpful to use a magic word so students don't move or talk until you're done giving directions. Choose a silly word like "pepperoni" or a fun vocabulary word and teach students not to lift a finger until they hear you say it. For example: "When you hear the magic word which is? [class says "pepperoni"], you're going to get out your math journal, pencil, and eraser. [Pause] Pepperoni." Many students will listen intently to everything you say in anticipation of hearing the magic word, and you can let kids take turns choosing the magic word of the week to keep their interest up.

Another strategy is to find creative ways to have students repeat directions back to you. I like to switch it up to keep kids on their toes. Sometimes I'll say, "Tell your partner what the directions are for this activity" and hold up 10 fingers, slowly putting my fingers down one at a time until I'm at zero, then release students to begin the activity. Other times, I'll have students repeat the directions back to me in unison: "I need you to take out your book and turn to page 67. Which page? [67] Thank you, go ahead." I've also known teachers who give students a moment of silence to think about the directions and visualize themselves following through.

I'm sure you already know it's a good idea to write important information on the board, but I encourage you to do it consistently and make sure you put the info in the same place every time. Whenever you mention a page number, a time limit, or any other detail students are likely to forget, make a note of it in a designated section of your board. Then you can simply point to the board or poster instead of repeating yourself. Many students find this extremely helpful, and over time, they will learn to check the board before asking you to give the directions again.

I also like to use a backwards countdown or timer to keep things moving. Isn't it funny how something as simple as cleaning up paper scraps can take ten minutes if you allow it to drag on? The timer is your best friend. Tell kids they've got two minutes to get everything put away and be prepared for the next activity. You can use a real timer and put it under a document camera for students to see, or project an online timer or timer app on your interactive whiteboard to display the countdown.

For really short time periods, countdown verbally and show the amount on your hands: "When I get to zero, I need you to have your backpack on and be ready to line up. 10, 9, 8..." When time is up, move on to the next activity just like you said you'd do, and let stragglers catch up without acknowledging them except to quietly help as needed. If you're consistent with this, students will learn you mean what you say and they have to keep pace!

Another great technique is to give students a purpose for following the directions. If you want kids to open their novels in preparation for a discussion, say, "In a moment, you're going to turn to page 214 and find the word *quintessential.* I'd like you to put your finger on that word and be prepared to talk about what it means in the context of the paragraph. Ready? Okay, begin. Page 214. I'll know you're ready when I see your finger on the word *quintessential.*" Similarly, if you want groups of students to prepare for a science experiment, ask them to assemble the materials they need and hold up a specific item when they've found it–they'll work more quickly because they won't want to be the last group ready.

Do less talking yourself and get kids talking more

One of the most tiring parts of teaching is having to talk all day long. In the next chapter, I'll share some ways you can turn the learning over to kids, and on the surface, that seems like a pretty straightforward way to solve the problem of too much teacher talk. If you use fewer teacher-directed activities, the kids will naturally do more talking and you can take a backseat, right?

But it doesn't necessarily work that way. I've found myself talking almost constantly during group work and student-directed projects because I'm trying to push kids' thinking, provide feedback, and help them stay on-task. Even when the learning has been turned over to students, it's still tempting to spend too much time giving directions, repeating important information, and telling students how they did instead of asking them to reflect on their work.

Try teaching students signals for your often-repeated phrases and for transitions. Cut down on conversations about drinks of water and pencil sharpening by showing kids how to use sign language to request permission, then use sign language to indicate your answer back: *yes, no,* or *wait.* I also like to teach kids sign language for *please, thank you,* and *you're welcome* so that I can reinforce their good choices without constantly talking. Or, use a chime, music, or other auditory signal to indicate when it's time to start an activity, pause, and clean up. All of these strategies give kids a break from hearing your voice: they are far more likely to tune in to a unique sound than to a twenty word directive.

It's also helpful to move away from the front of the classroom. It's easy to get in an instructional rut when you stand at the same place near the board all day long. Try occasionally sitting on the side of the classroom or in an absent student's desk and say, "I need someone to go up and demonstrate ___ for us."

Because students are used to the person at the board facilitating the lesson, the volunteer is likely to talk for much longer than if you stand at the front and he's in his seat answering you. You can even remain sitting among the class once the student is done demonstrating, and ask follow up questions from other students instead of commenting on the student's demo yourself (*What do you all think? Is that an effective method? How do you know? Does anyone use a different strategy? Would you go up and show us?*)

When giving feedback to kids, try turning your statements into questions and prompts. Instead of saying to a group, *Nice work over there, I like the strategy you used for ___,* ask the kids to reflect on their own work: *Tell me how your group has chosen to solve ___.* Instead of telling a child, *Take a look at #3—that answer is incorrect,* say, *Would you tell me how you got the answer for #3?* Not only will these questions get students talking instead of you, kids will also have the chance to reflect on and articulate their learning.

Always be on the lookout for moments when you summarize or review for students, and make a conscious decision to get their input instead. If you hear yourself saying *once again, remember, as I said, as always, so to sum this up,* or *don't forget,* that probably means you're about to drive home an important point for the second or third (or tenth) time.

Try making those moments a chance for kids to share by saying: *What's the rule about this? Who can sum this section up for us? Who remembers the way to determine ___?* Some teachers even turn those moments into interactive exercises in which the whole class does a hand motion, body movement, sound, or chant to indicate that they're summarizing an idea or reviewing directions before getting started.

We rarely get an insightful response when asking things like, *Are you guys getting this?* so we either move on without kids understanding or we repeat something we've already said. Try inviting kids to put what you've explained into their own words, either repeating it back to you or turning and talking to a partner. So instead of asking, *Does that make sense?* say, *Can you put that in your own words?*

Perhaps most importantly, don't steal the struggle. It can be uncomfortable to watch passively as kids figure out an answer, but they often need time and silence so they can think. Resist the urge to talk students through every step of a problem, and instead just observe.

I often worry about keeping the momentum of a lesson going, and it's hard for me to allow several moments of silent "wait time" or "think time" before calling on students. However, I try to push against the feeling that I will lose students' attention because I know providing wait time can actually increase the length and quality of their responses. Letting kids think instead of rushing in to narrate or question them will build anticipation around what's going to be said next and increase participation as more kids are prepared to move into the conversation.

Use questions to redirect behavior instead of nagging

A lot of the talking most of us do throughout the day is related to student behavior, and most of the time, we're wasting our breath. It's far more effective (not to mention easier and less disruptive) to give students "the teacher look" and keep the lesson moving. If you need to have a conversation about the behavior with a student or issue a consequence, try to wait for a break in your instruction rather than stop the whole class from learning while you discipline one kid.

When our goal is constructing a self-running classroom, we must resist the urge to lecture students every time someone forgets their materials, interrupts, or makes an inappropriate noise. It's an endless trap—kids already know what they should be doing, so they tune us out when we nag them. We say it again, they ignore it again. And we go home at the end of the day exhausted because we've spent our time trying to control kids' behavior instead of equipping them to exercise self-control.

One of the simplest tricks I've learned for breaking this cycle is to give students the responsibility for solving the problem. I try to ask questions that require the child to think about what she or he is doing and determine a more appropriate behavior.

For example, instead of saying, *Put that away!* I'll ask, *Where should that paper be?* Instead of *Get in line!* I'll ask, *How should you be standing right now?* Instead of *Spit out that gum!* I'll ask, *What is our rule about chewing gum?* My absolute favorite question, which works in just about any situation, is: *What should you be doing right now?*

Usually when I ask these types of questions, students will pause, think, and then self-correct without any problems. The questions work well because I haven't given a command for kids to rebel against: they haven't had to give in because they were never told what to do. *Students* determine the solution and choose a different behavior, and I get to say something positive and encouraging (like "good choice" or "thanks for fixing that") instead of wearing us both down with more nagging.

Of course, not all questions inspire self-reliance and problem solving. Many times we ask "why" questions that are really commands in disguise. I can't count the number of times I've asked students, *Why do I hear talking?* when I really mean, *Stop that right now!*

In those moments, I've already decided there's no good reason for anyone to be talking, so I don't really want to hear what's causing it or get into a debate with the kids about whether the talking is justified. So, I try to replace those unproductive "why" questions with words that inspire constructive responses from students and help them think about their behavioral choices.

Why are you out of your seat again? becomes *Where should you be right now?*

Why are you pushing her? becomes *Where should your hands be?*

Why are you sitting there doing nothing? becomes *What should you be working on?*

The idea is to avoid questions that students can't really answer without arguing or defending themselves, and ask legitimate questions which prompt kids to think and get back on task.

Empower kids to solve their own interpersonal disputes

Social and personal issues between students can be a huge distraction in the classroom and cause you to lose your focus and enthusiasm. Nothing makes me want to pack up and go home more than spending hours developing a fantastic activity on a super important concept...and then having all that energy derailed by cries of, *"She bumped me! He took my pencil! Stoppppp, that's miiiiine!"*

So, an important part of constructing a self-running classroom that frees you to teach is extracting yourself from minor social disputes between kids. Resist the urge to solve problems by pronouncing who is right, who is wrong, and what students need to do next.

Instead, model social problem-solving skills explicitly and repeatedly. Each time there's a dispute at the beginning of the school year, talk kids through it while the rest of the class listens. It's better to lose instructional time on this for a few weeks than to allow arguing to disrupt your lessons for the rest of the year.

Always put the ball in the students' court. If someone says, "My partner is refusing to work with me," respond with, "What can you say to her?" Observe what happens, guide students to solve problems together, and reinforce appropriate choices. You can also say, "Go ahead, talk to him again—I'll watch," which is helpful if students have already argued and not gotten anywhere, or if the child is too intimidated to stand up to the other child independently. (I've written out a complete script you can use and some if-then scenarios in my classroom management book, *The Cornerstone*.)

If you are consistent with this, students will stop expecting you to referee every minor disagreement. They will learn to identify the serious situations in which you need to be involved, and realize you are not going to administer swift justice in petty situations, so it's quicker and simpler to try working things out themselves first.

I also recommend that you find the kids in your class who are well-respected by their peers and skilled at solving interpersonal problems, and designate them as your Mediators. This should be a prestigious role in your classroom that students clamor to prove themselves worthy of. If a group of students need help determining their roles in a team assignment and you're busy assisting another group, ask your Mediator to help out. The Mediator should be trained to do the same thing you do: ask questions, encourage independent problem solving, and assist kids in finding resolutions rather than telling them what to do.

Let go of the need for control

You can probably see how letting go of control is at the core of everything we've discussed so far in the chapter. After all, micromanaging a classroom is exhausting. It will lead to burnout! I encourage you to think very, very carefully about how prominent of a role you need to play in the minor aspects of how your classroom is run:

Do you need students to ask permission every time they want to use the bathroom and get a drink, or can you create a sign-out sheet?

Do students need to raise their hands before throwing away trash, or can you teach them to do so without asking at the end of the period on their way out the door?

Do you need to monitor the supply of paper, sharpened pencils, and so on, or can you have a student do that job as part of your classroom helper system?

Only you know the answers to those questions—there's no right or wrong here. I'm simply suggesting that you consider the amount of energy you're expending on controlling things in your classroom that students could theoretically take over themselves.

As you build a classroom community and learn to trust your students, you will become more comfortable with allowing them to make decisions and exercise personal freedom. Over time, their responsibility for classroom logistics will increase and yours will decrease, creating a truly self-running classroom.

15

Motivate students to take charge of their learning

You've spent hours creating a super engaging lesson that you just know your students will love. You've brought in all the materials, set them up, and launched into a learning experience you're sure the kids will be thrilled to participate in.

But the reaction isn't what you expected. The students just sit there passively, halfway listening to you. A handful of kids answer your questions, but no one is asking any questions of their own. You're running yourself ragged trying to get kids excited about learning, but they're not buying in. They're completing the assignment you gave them without thinking deeply about their answers. They're just not engaged or reflecting carefully on what they're doing.

In short, the students have not taken charge of their own learning. They wouldn't be doing the assignment if you, the teacher, weren't telling them to do it.

We've all experienced many lessons like these, and they're not very fun to teach *or* learn. In this chapter, I want to share some ways that you can empower your students to take ownership of their learning and become truly invested in what happens in the classroom.

What are you doing in your classroom now that you could turn over to your students to do themselves?

That's a question once posed by Alan November, and I think it's a fantastic starting point when you're deciding how to empower students to take charge of their own learning.

Maybe your students are stuck in a rut with spelling—the weekly spelling test is a prescribed part of your curriculum that you have to implement, but it's just not working. You're constantly trying to think of new and creative ways to have kids write their spelling words. You're nagging kids to complete their spelling homework, and using up valuable class time giving spelling tests. Meanwhile, the kids are just going through the motions, scribbling down their words five times each but never transferring what they learned about spelling rules to their actual writing.

So, let's place the problem within the context of the student-directed learning question: *How could you turn over spelling lists, practice, and/or assessment to your students to do themselves?*

Maybe the kids could have a say in choosing their spelling words. They could (regularly or once a month) proofread each other's writing and make notes on frequently misspelled words, compiling them into spelling lists. If you're required to use a set list of words, students could choose two of their own frequently-misspelled words to add to the pre-determined list.

Maybe, instead of giving spelling tests yourself, you could have students give one another their tests, allowing them to take turns reading the words to a partner or small group. This would free you up to do better things with your time than stand at the front of the room, reading out a list of spelling words every Friday. It would also give your students more exposure to the spelling words and permit them to take a more active and enjoyable role in the assessment process...especially if they're able to grade the test (their own or their partner's) afterward.

Maybe you could have students who excel at a particular spelling rule give the class a 3-5 minute mini-lesson. This could be an earned privilege that students are given once they've demonstrated mastery.

Or maybe you could enlist students' help in choosing ways for them to practice their spelling words for homework: see what creative ideas they come up with, and give them choices or spelling menus so they can select which type of practice they'd prefer to complete.

Can you see the possibilities here? How much more motivated would you be to teach mundane aspects of your curriculum like spelling if you were using these strategies? And how much more motivated would your students be to learn how to spell? Any topic instantly becomes more fun and meaningful for *everyone* involved when the kids are given some ownership of how they learn.

Your most powerful tool for turning learning over to students

I believe technology is the most powerful tool you have for giving kids ownership of their learning. Computers and tablets can provide infinite options for both content consumption and content creation. Programs and apps can offer personalized learning paths for students, tracking kids' progress and adjusting the next practice session accordingly. I believe that the quality and variety of tools available is going to continue increasing to the point where even the most tech-averse teacher will be saying, *How did I ever teach without this?*

Even if you only have a few half-working computers in your classroom, technology can still help provide more choices, and that means you can use it to empower students to take charge of their learning. Start with just one or two tech tools in one or two subject areas. Some teachers I've coached like to plan new ways to use technology for just a single unit of study each quarter. They choose one topic during the quarter and actively look for ways to give kids more ownership over that content using technology.

If this is an approach that's workable for you, think back on those dull areas of curriculum you identified earlier, and consider how technology might provide some new options for making the learning more engaging for students.

If you're not particularly tech-savvy, you can use *content consumption tools* at first. Have kids watch videos online, read eBooks, research on websites, or use Google Earth to tour faraway places. When you feel ready, choose one or two resources that are a bit more interactive, such as webquests, games, or online quizzes.

Once you're comfortable with implementing those, try adding at least one *content creation tool* in which students use technology to create and share information with others. Kids could use free apps like I Tell a Story or Toontastic to collaboratively share what they've learned. Students can also create podcasts, upload videos to a class blog, Skype with other classes or communities, or create a digital poster through Glogster.

Pick one app or website that appeals to you and try it out! You don't have to comb through every program that's out there and find the perfect one, and you don't have to introduce a new tool with every unit of study. Many kids thrive off of familiarity and get a real confidence boost from becoming proficient with a tool, so don't feel pressured to constantly introduce something new and exciting.

Instead, pick a content creation tool that is open-ended and revisit it throughout the year. Your students could use Voicethread, for example, to share what they learned using video, audio, and/or text. The tool is so versatile that you could use it at any grade level for any subject area, and creating just one Voicethread a month or even a quarter can be a powerful learning experience.

Personalize learning with student-directed projects

If all kids are learning the same thing at the same time in the same way, guess who owns that learning? We call that "teacher-directed" for a reason, right? So if you want kids to be more motivated, try incorporating more *student*-directed activities.

The term "personalized student learning" has become a big buzzword in education, and it's not as daunting as it sounds. Personalization is about allowing students to pursue their own interests related to a standard you're teaching, and a great way to do that is through student-directed projects.

The purpose of a student-directed project is for kids to take ownership of a topic they're studying. It's different from a traditional project in which all students learn about the same thing the same way and produce very similar end products. With student-directed projects, kids choose an aspect of a topic they're interested in, and are given some choice as to how they explore that topic as well as how they share the information they've learned.

Because a lack of time is one of the biggest obstacles in conducting student-directed projects, I've tried to plan just one each month. I rotate through the subject areas so that students do a math project in September, a social studies project in October, a science project in November, and so on. That usually means by the end of the school year, the kids have completed two student-directed projects in each subject area.

The projects don't have to be complicated or consume a lot of class time. One of my favorite student-directed projects is a spring project I created for our second grade unit on animal habitats. Each child chose an animal to research and an essential question she or he wanted to understand about how that animal adapts to its environment. The kids used library books and internet resources to conduct their research and took notes on a form I provided, then put that information together into a presentation style of their choice. I gave them a list of formats which they'd tried previously in the school year and were already familiar with: mini-books, posters, digital posters, slide presentations, Prezis, skits, videos, etc.

Though I could have easily allotted 20 hours or more to this project, I had a lot of other things to teach in science and had to limit it. I'd estimate that in total, students spent about 6 hours of class time on the animal adaptations project. They worked on it in the afternoons during the week of benchmark testing (in other words, at a time when they were mentally drained in the morning and needed a more developmentally appropriate and enjoyable activity in the afternoon.) Their class presentations occurred one afternoon after a pep rally when it would have been difficult to get much else done.

I think it was far more valuable for students to see their peers present on different animal adaptations than to simply read about them in our text. As an added bonus, I got to facilitate as students pursued their own learning instead of telling them what to learn and giving them the information myself. Now *that* is energizing, enjoyable teaching!

In recent years, many teachers have experimented with taking student-directed projects to a new level through 20% Time. The term originated with Google's 20% policy, in which employees are allowed to use twenty percent of their working hours to pursue a project of their own choosing. In the classroom, 20% Time is a portion of the school day or week in which students are allowed to pick their own projects or even learning outcomes.

Some teachers keep this very structured, and require students to use the project to work toward the standards and skills for their grade level. Other teachers use more of an open-ended format (often called Genius Hour) which allows kids to choose "passion projects" and explore any topic they're really interested in. You can visit GeniusHour.com to learn more about the practicalities of these projects and how to implement them in your own classroom.

Give self-assessments for kids to reflect on their own progress

Assessment is so time- and labor-intensive for teachers and generally not very meaningful for students. We spend hours correcting every mistake and writing detailed comments on assignments only for kids to stuff the papers in their backpacks and never give them a second look.

However, when you turn the assessment over to students, they become personally invested in it. They develop a deeper understanding of how they're being graded. And, they have the opportunity to reflect on their own progress instead of waiting for an adult to tell them how they did.

One of the easiest ways to incorporate student self-assessment is by having kids staple a copy of the grading rubric to their projects, essays, and other assignments before turning their work in. They can use a pencil to circle where they think they fall on the scale, and write comments explaining why they believe they've earned that score.

When you're ready to grade the assignments, the rubric is already there and you can simply use a pen to circle the student's final grade. You'll get a really clear picture of how well students understand their own strengths and weaknesses, and gather important documentation for conferences.

For assignments that don't have a rubric, ask students to self-evaluate by writing one or two sentences. They can respond to prompts such as: *The easiest part of this task was ___; The hardest part was ___; I thought I did a good job with ___; I need more practice with ___.* Kids can also evaluate cooperative learning assignments, reflecting on what they contributed to the group and how they can improve their teamwork skills.

I strongly recommend that you enlist students' help in creating the grading criteria. Show anonymous exemplar assignments from previous years' classes and talk about what makes them fantastic, writing down what students observe. Then show other benchmark examples and have students explain what makes those examples weaker. Use kids' observations to develop criteria for each point of a simple rubric or grading scale: *What makes this example an A? How is a C different? What would an F look like?*

When you create grading criteria together, students not only have a better understanding of how they're being assessed, but they're also more likely to buy into the assessment process. The methods of grading become meaningful instead of arbitrary. Kids start to recognize excellence and can tell when they're submitting work that is subpar. The class time you dedicate to involving students in the assessment process will almost always pay itself back threefold.

Another way to give kids ownership of the assessment process is through bi-weekly work samples. Send graded work home every 2 weeks, and give kids the chance to look through the work before you send it. Have students fill out a reflection form, completing sentences such as:

I am most proud of ___ because ___.
Last time I wanted to improve ___.
When I consider how I've done in this area in the last 2 weeks, I think ___.
I would like to improve ___. To do this, I plan to ___.

You can read more about this process and see the related forms at www.unshakeablebook.com.

Conduct student-led conferences with kids' parents

One year I taught at a school that was so overcrowded, two classes of students were assigned to share a single classroom. All day, every day, it was me and my 28 students and another teacher and her 27 students. Yep, nearly 60 people sharing one classroom!

The situation could have been a complete disaster, but fortunately my co-teacher was incredible and taught me so many great tips and tricks. One of the best things I learned from her was how to conduct student-led conferences.

I remember being incredibly anxious about one particular conference because we were going to have to tell a parent that her child was in danger of being retained because he wasn't putting forth any effort in his work. My co-teacher said to me, "What are you nervous about? *We're* not telling the parent that, the kid is!" And she sat that child right down at the conference table with us and proceeded to ask him questions like these:

How do you think you've been doing in class?
What areas do you think need improvement?
Why do you think that?
How has your homework been going?
Can you explain why you haven't been doing it?
What about class time—can you show your mom your notes?
I see very few notes—would you tell us what's happening with that?
How is all of this affecting your grades?
What do you think will happen if your grades don't improve?
What needs to change in order for you to do better?
How can your teachers help you be more successful?
How can mom and dad help?
What is our plan moving forward, starting today, to help you improve?

Those are pretty deep questions for an eight-year-old, but the child did a remarkable job responding. I remember sitting at that table absolutely astounded that neither I nor my co-teacher had to say anything negative about the child to his mother. We did not criticize, shame, tell on, or scold him.

The whole conversation revolved around the child reflecting on his choices and then determining what he would do to improve...in front of three witnesses who were going to hold him accountable! We made no accusations and said nothing that the parent could throw in our faces later or complain to the principal about. Instead, we'd learned a lot about how the student viewed his school performance and the things that were distracting him and holding him back. We were able to end the conference with a firm plan for improvement that everyone present was fully invested in.

I've used the student-led conference model ever since that day, and have found that both parents and students love doing them. You can find more information at unshakeablebook.com, including a free printable student-led conference sheet with the questions I use to guide most conferences from start to finish.

A surefire way to tell if students own the learning

It can be difficult to tell whether kids are really self-directed in their learning. Sometimes true student ownership means working quietly; other times, it means loud and enthusiastic participation. Sometimes it means working alone; other times, it means collaborating with others.

One way to tell who owns the learning is to observe who is asking the questions. If the teacher is doing all the questioning and the students are just answering, it's possible the kids are being busy or compliant but are not truly taking ownership of what's happening in the classroom.

However, when children ask *why, how, what happens if,* and *couldn't we try,* you can be sure they are thinking deeply about the topic and are invested in their own learning.

We can encourage kids to be more curious in the classroom and ask and answer their own questions by explicitly teaching the art of asking questions. We can also model questioning behaviors for them, and encourage kids when they do ask questions. The behaviors that we draw attention to in the classroom often get repeated, so pointing out the good questions that kids ask and helping them pursue the answers is powerful.

Wait—doesn't turning the learning over to students actually create *more* work for me?

Yes, sometimes it does, especially in the short term. Creating projects and teaching kids how to direct their own learning takes a lot more time than photocopying and passing out worksheets. But turning the learning over to students will save you time and energy in the long run.

Once you've created a set of project guidelines, you can reuse and adapt them over and over again during your teaching career.

Once you've taught kids to be independent, you will spend less time repeating yourself and going over your expectations.

And once you've helped kids find a real sense of meaning and purpose in their learning, you will find that they are more actively engaged and excited to learn…and that means they're *giving* you energy instead of just taking it.

Slowly offer students more choice and input as to what they do in the classroom. Keep looking for strategies to meet individual needs. Find ways to allow kids to pursue their own unique interests, and you'll see their motivation levels grow exponentially.

16

Connect with kids and gain energy instead of letting them drain you

Have you noticed that teachers and students often behave very differently from one another at the end of the school day? Teachers are usually ready to collapse in a heap on the floor from exhaustion, while students are bouncing off the walls, racing down the hallways to their busses, and brimming with excitement.

You may not have ever thought about *why* it happens that way. But the reason is actually pretty simple...and you can address it immediately. It all has to do with your classroom energy flow.

Change the flow of energy from one way to reciprocal

Teachers often spend their days giving of themselves endlessly to students while the kids just sit and absorb (or deflect, in some cases!) The flow of energy is one way so that students are the constant recipients and have an excess at the end of the day.

They sit still and listen while the teacher presents; they half-heartedly complete assignments while the teacher musters up the enthusiasm to praise and encourage; they goof off while the teacher paces around the room redirecting behavior and trying to keep the entire show running smoothly. If you want to avoid burnout, *you cannot let that happen.*

There are two important ways you can gain energy from students instead of just giving it all away. One key (which we explored in the previous chapter) is to get kids actively involved in their learning so they're doing just as much work—or even more—than you are.

When students are motivated to take charge of the learning process, they are able to channel their excess energy into pursuits that matter. As their teacher, you become re-energized from watching the learning process in action and interacting with kids who are enthusiastic about their work. The flow of energy in the classroom becomes reciprocal as you motivate them, and they in turn motivate you.

The other key to gaining energy from kids is to intentionally connect with your students and enjoy their company. Let's explore some ways to build those relationships.

The secret to being a happy lifelong educator

The relationships you have with students are really the crux of whether or not you enjoy teaching. The kids are the ones you spend most of your time with at work, and how much you like being around them is directly correlated to your job satisfaction.

When you can learn to tune out all of the distractions that pull you away from connecting with and enjoying your students, you'll have figured out the secret to being a happy lifelong educator.

After all, if you don't enjoy the kids, what's left? The meetings? The paperwork? The testing? The kids *have* to be your greatest source of enjoyment as an educator.

If you believe this is true and experience that enjoyment on a regular basis, I hope this chapter gives you some new ideas for strengthening those relationships and enjoying your students even more.

If you believe that relationships with kids are important but think you don't have time to foster them, this chapter is for you, too. Most suggestions take little or no time away from instruction and don't require much additional work on your part.

And if you believe that connecting with kids is important but you're so bogged down with their behavioral issues that sometimes the kids feel like the *worst* part of the job? It's okay to admit that. I've been there. This chapter is for you, too, because it's full of ways to help you see the good in your students and grab small moments of happiness and satisfaction from interacting with them.

Begin each day with individual connections

The first few minutes of the morning have the potential to set the tone for your entire school day. Therefore, it's very important to tune into your students right away and notice how they're feeling. If a student is seething with rage from a fight on the bus or feeling sad about something that happened at home the night before, you want to uncover that fact and address it *before* your instruction begins.

Try to stand in the doorway and greet your students as they enter the classroom each morning. Give kids the opportunity to engage in a casual conversation with you and talk about anything that's on their minds. Study their faces and body language carefully, and try to notice who might need some extra attention or positive reinforcement that day.

You can also create a greeting routine as part of your morning meeting. This will allow every person in the class to greet one another by name...and it can take as little as one minute!

Here's how it works. At the start of our morning meeting (Pledge of Allegiance, announcements, calendar, etc.), students gathered on the rug and I set a timer for one minute. The entire class then stood up and greeted one another, usually with a handshake style of their choosing. We practiced making eye contact and greeting each other by name, so students looked at each other, smiled, and took turns saying, "Good morning, ___!" before turning to repeat the gesture with another classmate. Sometimes I'd teach them how to say "hello" or "good morning" in another language, or they'd greet each other in a silly voice, which was always fun for them. When the timer went off, everyone sat back down.

In that single minute, students got to be acknowledged by almost every one of their peers as well as their teacher. Not only did this create a sense of community for the kids, but it did a world of good for me, too. Having every student smile up at me, shake my hand, and say, "Good morning, Mrs. Watson!" set the tone for the entire day and reminded me that I am teaching students, not standards.

Learn at least one thing about every kid

One of the toughest things about building relationships with students is that there are so many of them and only one of you. Getting to know each child individually may feel impossible, especially if you teach multiple classes and have 150 kids (or more) on your roster.

Make it your goal to start with learning one thing about every student. That's a completely doable goal! You can't know *everything* about every kid, but you can know *one* thing about every kid.

Some students will reveal their inner workings within the first five minutes of meeting you. They are the easy ones. Pay attention to your quiet and introverted students, and encourage them to share, too. Then use those insights to help you build a deeper relationship.

If a child is great at drawing, ask if he's drawn any sketches he'd like to share with you. If you know a student likes basketball, ask her if she watched the game last night, or tell her about a funny commercial with a famous basketball player and how it made you think of her.

Make a connection with 5 kids every day

If you find that you only have time to pay one-on-one attention to kids when they're doing something wrong, this strategy is for you. No more giving only negative attention to your challenging students, or overlooking the kids who usually make good choices!

Here's what you do: download my free Daily Connections form from unshakeablebook.com, or just divide your class list into fifths. Each group of students will be assigned a day of the week. If you have 25 kids in your class, that means you'll have 5 targeted kids for Monday, 5 for Tuesday, and so on.

Each day, look at your list and see which kids you need to pay extra attention to that day. You could even pray for those students or think positive thoughts for them, if you choose.

When the class is working independently, spend a little more time giving feedback to those kids. Compliment them on things you might otherwise overlook because you're so busy. Observe them more closely when they're working, and give a smile or thumbs up to encourage them to keep at it. At dismissal, ask them about their weekend plans.

You might also use that day to spend a little more time reading through and responding to those 5 kids' writing assignments. You can learn a lot by what students say in their journals! Take the time to write back, asking a few questions and making encouraging comments. You can also make a note for yourself about things kids have written so you remember to bring it up in conversation later.

Of course, students should never know that you have a system for connecting with them. The daily connections list is only for your reference, and you certainly don't want to ignore the other kids! The goal is to have a routine that makes it easier for you to make sure you're sending a critical message to each and every student through the smallest of gestures: *I see you. You matter. I acknowledge you as a unique, individual person in this classroom, and I care about you.*

Start a "Sharing Time" or "Good Things Time"

Keep this simple and informal with older kids: you can set aside a few minutes once or twice a week (such as Monday morning or Friday afternoon) and allow students to share some good news from their lives. Many high school teachers I know recommend this as an easy way to get to know the kids a little better and celebrate their successes.

If you have oral language goals in your learning standards, Sharing Time is one of the most fun and productive ways to address them, and you can make the process a little more structured. Sharing Time was the highlight of the day for my third graders, and it was actually standards-based.

The routine is similar to Show and Tell, except the focus is only on sharing what's happening in the kids' lives. There's no need to bring in a material possession: students can share what they did the evening before, upcoming vacation plans, a movie they watched, or even a dream they had (believe it or not, this was a very popular topic for my students, and the other kids hung on their every word!) They can only bring in items if they have special permission (which is granted if the object is integral to the story) so the kids understand this is not about showing off all their cool toys.

I assigned each child a day of the week, so if I had 25 kids in my class, 5 kids would share each day. Most shares only lasted a minute or two, but if they went long, I'd gently prompt the sharer to ask for audience participation: each child took three questions or comments after their share to facilitate conversation skills and develop oral language.

I've held sharing time at various points during the day: some years, I did it during morning meetings as a community-building exercise. One year, I had three and half straight hours with students in the morning and was permitted to have a 10 minute snack time to break that up, so we did sharing while the kids ate. Other years, I did Sharing Time during dismissal to encourage students to pack up quickly and get settled back down to listen.

I learned so much about my students and their families through Sharing Time. It was a lovely opportunity for all of us to focus on the individual members of our classroom community.

Surprise kids with compliment slips and appreciation notes

Many of the public elementary schools where I taught in South Florida encourage students to wear uniforms. However, the policy is rarely enforced, and in my experience, about 70% of the kids wear uniforms and the other 30% wear what they want, even though free uniforms are generally furnished by the PTA for families in need. This always bugged me as a teacher because I don't like asking kids to do things I can't enforce, and I felt the lack of consequences was unfair to the kids who diligently wore their uniforms.

I tried talking with my students about why the uniform policy was in place and how it benefited them as well as the school community. I tried giving polite reminders to parents. I tried questioning kids about their lack of uniforms. And, I tried far more nagging than was actually productive. Eventually I decided that this wasn't a battle I was willing to fight (especially since the principal wasn't going to back me up), and I left the subject alone.

One day I overhead a child saying to another, "I wish I didn't have to wear my uniform, but my mom says it's the right thing to do." That's when it hit me—instead of focusing on the kids who weren't complying with the policy, I should spend my time and energy on those who *were*.

I typed the sentence "Thank you for wearing your uniform" and copy/pasted it 10 times on the same page, then printed out a few copies and cut them apart into strips. The next day, I made a mental note of who was in uniform, and when the students went to music class, I placed the notes on their desks.

The kids absolutely beamed when they returned to the classroom. I told them it was just a little way to let them know I noticed they were doing the right thing, even if I didn't usually mention it. Nothing was said to the kids who were out of uniform and they simply shrugged and took out their materials for our lesson.

I didn't give it much more thought until I realized two kids who typically wore jeans came to school the next day in uniform. "You look handsome today—that uniform looks good on you!" I said with genuine delight. The following week, another child appeared in uniform. Although I'd told the kids not to expect the notes on a regular basis ("You never know which day you might get one!"), I made sure to pass them out that day!

My class went from about 70% uniform compliant to 95%…on any given day, only one or two kids would be out of uniform. And the same thing happened the following year, and the year after that. Other teachers would stop me in the hall and say, "How do you get so many of your kids to wear their uniforms?" The truth was that I did nothing more than acknowledge my students' right choices. They knew I cared about uniforms, and because we had a strong rapport, that made them care, too.

I typed up all sorts of thank you notes for the kids: *Thank you for being on time to school. Thank you for doing your homework consistently.*

Thank you for returning signed forms the very next day. Sometimes I only gave a slip to one child when I noticed a particularly positive behavior: *Thank you for being so helpful in the classroom. Thank you for being a good friend to your classmate. Thank you for doing the right thing when no one was looking.*

The notes meant more to some kids than others, of course. Some kids just read them and threw them away. Some kids took them home to show their parents. And at least one child kept every single note displayed behind the clear plastic cover of her homework binder and admired them every time she got her assignments out.

I've made fancier versions of the compliment slips now—you can get them from unshakeablebook.com if you don't want to make your own. They're such an easy and quick way to acknowledge students, and the process allows you to gain energy from the kids who are doing the right thing instead of expending your energy on the kids who are doing the wrong thing.

Hold laid-back parties and special events

I hope your school permits you to have classroom parties at least once or twice a year. Most of my principals only allowed Valentine's Day and end-of-year parties, so it was tempting to fall into the trap of going all out and over-planning for those very rare occasions.

After a few stressful events, I realized most kids are thrilled just to get a break from the regular routine and workload. I didn't need to have 5 different games and activities, a spread of food that would feed an army, and so on...especially when the stress of overseeing everything put me in a bad mood and caused me to snap at the kids instead of celebrating with them.

I've found it's better to focus on creating a time in which you and the kids can relax and enjoy each other's company. If it's a warm day, you could hold the entire celebration outside, make ice cream sundaes, and spend some time hanging out together on the playground or basketball court. On a cold or rainy day, play a favorite movie for the kids and order some pizzas. You have no idea how much it will mean to some of your students if you sit down with them to eat instead of grading papers at your desk. It might be the only time all month in which they can talk to you about whatever they want and not be pressured to get back on task.

You could also surprise the kids by *participating* in a simple game instead of just facilitating it. I once joined a game of Four Corners during my class' end-of-year party. Afterward, I wondered why I had spent every indoor recess trying to control the game, catch the cheaters, and keep kids from getting too silly instead of just having fun with them! I missed out on so much—it was more fun for them *and* for me when I let loose and played the game, too.

The bottom line is that holidays and parties should be fun for everyone involved. A stressed out, exhausted teacher is not fun for the kids. My advice is to go all out for those celebrations only if that's something you can handle, enjoy, and do with a good attitude.

Acknowledge birthdays in a creative way

Birthdays are the perfect time to make individual connections with students, and it can be a relatively simple undertaking if you plan out a good system in advance. I will admit I am terrible about remembering students' birthdays, so this was something I had to be very intentional about.

I bought a small laminated birthday poster with all the months on it, and each year, I used Vis-A-Vis markers to write each of the kids' names under the appropriate month. I then established a yearlong class job called The Birthday Helper. I assigned this task to a highly responsible child with an excellent memory and a self-starter type of personality.

The Birthday Helper was in charge of erasing students' names when they transferred out of our classroom, as well as figuring out the birthdays of new students and adding them to the poster. The Birthday Helper was also responsible for telling me at dismissal time if there were any student birthdays the following day, and helping me prepare the classroom with whatever birthday celebration I had decided to do that school year.

One of my favorite easy ways to acknowledge kids' birthdays was with a no-homework pass. I tucked it inside a homemade card: a piece of construction paper folded in half that the whole class had signed during morning work. Some years I also gave the birthday boy or girl the opportunity to sit in a special chair for the day (beanbag, stool, swivel chair, or my desk chair.)

I know a teacher who lets her students call "recess" on their birthday at any one point in the day. The entire class stops what they're doing, sings "Happy Birthday", and gets a 10 minute indoor recess time.

I also know of teachers who wrap the top of the birthday child's desk with wrapping paper, give a "sit with a friend" pass, or allow the birthday child to read a favorite book to the class (or have a family member come in to read it.)

Another idea is to use the birthday child's picture as your computer desktop background and display it on your interactive whiteboard. You can use a free site like FaceInHole.com to create a silly image or an image reflective of the child's interests. I recommend doing this with your own picture first, and asking kids if they're comfortable with you doing the same for them on their birthdays. Some kids might be embarrassed by it and prefer a photo of something else they like (a favorite singer, actor, sports player, etc.)

If you want to make the acknowledgement more personalized, have students fill out a get-to-know-you type of form in the beginning of the school year, and make sure kids share their favorite snack, drink, candy, etc. Collect all the forms and make one shopping trip per quarter. Your students will probably have forgotten about the form they filled out and will be shocked that you knew their favorite treats!

Though I think individual birthday acknowledgements are more meaningful (especially for young children), group celebrations might be more practical. You could hold a Birthday Breakfast at the beginning of the month for all students who have an upcoming birthday. Bring in treats and juice to share just before the first bell rings, or even during morning work time (getting to skip the pledge and announcements can be a big deal to kids.) You can also use the Birthday Breakfast as a learning opportunity: encourage healthy eating by providing nutritious choices, and teach students how to properly set a table.

Start a Breakfast Club/Lunch Bunch/Snack Pack

Try to create an open-door policy so that students know they are welcome and safe in your classroom during lunch periods. I know several middle school teachers who make their classroom available with comfortable chairs and books from the class library. Students can sit and read, listen to music, and talk to friends or the teacher.

You can also create a system where a special lunch or snack time with you is offered as an occasional reward. An unstructured time to just sit and talk about what's going on in students' lives really endears you to them (and vice versa.)

If your students' desks are arranged in groups, you can award points to each team for a job well done (cooperative problem solving, communicating respectfully, staying on-task, etc.) Keep track of the points by making simple tally marks on your whiteboard. Each time a team gets to 20 points (or whatever predetermined number you choose), they get to eat lunch with you in the classroom. Afterward, erase the team's points and have them start again. Since teams are not in competition with each other, the other teams' points stay intact and they keep working toward their own special lunch.

If you're like me and *need* your lunch break to decompress, skip the Lunch Bunch and try meeting in a Snack Pack at another time during the day. Due to a late lunch slot most years, I let my students eat a snack in the classroom during our small group reading instruction. Every few weeks when a team earned 20 points, I'd pull them over to our small group table for 5 minutes at the beginning of the reading block while the rest of the kids got settled into their rotations. We'd eat a fun snack together and just chat as a team.

You could also try doing a quick Snack Pack while the rest of the class is working independently on an assignment, or right before dismissal. You could even try it 5 minutes before the first bell rings or during morning work/bell work/warm up activities, and call it a Breakfast Club.

These Lunch Bunch-type gatherings are a great way to have informal conversations with kids that are not related to school. You can learn a lot about your students' hobbies, families, and so on. Be sure to share info about yourself, too!

Make the most of every unstructured moment you get

With all the curriculum that must be taught on a daily basis, the only time for connecting with kids might be those unexpected or short moments we somehow manage to steal, so be on the lookout for every opportunity!

Try standing in the hallway during class changes and talking with kids as they walk by. If you're assigned recess, lunch, or dismissal duty, try to utilize that unstructured time, too. These are great opportunities to look for ways to see your students in a different light and connect with the children who are shy or otherwise not actively seeking your attention.

I once had a student who exhibited extreme behavior problems and was reading three years below grade level. As a result, most of our in-class interactions were not very much fun for either of us. But I'll never forget how it felt to see him on the basketball court at recess for the first time—he was the best player in the class. The smile on his face when he was in his element and experiencing success allowed me to see him as the unique, talented person he really was. I'd sometimes stand next to the court and cheer him on as he played, and I couldn't tell you which one of us enjoyed that more!

Some teachers play ball with their kids at recess or jump rope together. My style was to sit on a bench and talk with the kids. The kids would saunter over to me and say shyly, "Mrs. Watson—guess what!" We'd revel in the luxury I had of listening to their sweet, rambling stories about pets and loose teeth and video games without having to politely redirect them back to the work they were supposed to be doing.

If you have the ability to add *any* additional outdoor time to your schedule as an occasional reward for students, I urge you to jump at that opportunity and build it into your behavior management system. The fresh air and fun atmosphere will invigorate you and give kids the break they need in order to process their learning and prepare for more.

End each day with individual acknowledgments

You've probably heard the suggestion to give each student a "hug or a handshake" (their choice) as they leave the classroom each afternoon. A no-physical-contact variation is to simply stand at the door and smile as you say goodbye to each student by name.

If you haven't ever ended your day this way, I really encourage you to try it. This personal acknowledgement gives you one final chance to connect with each child, and I found the routine really calmed me down at the end of the day when I was feeling stressed. I loved knowing that whenever a student had a particularly rough time, I had the chance to wipe the slate clean and let him know I was ready for a fresh start: "Looking forward to tomorrow, John—I know you're going to have a great day!"

You can also use the end of the day to quickly compliment a child on anything you'd been meaning to say but just didn't have time to discuss ("Hey, that was such a great strategy you shared in math today, Kiana!" or "By the way, I saw the way you helped Melissa with her essay; thanks for being a good friend to her, Robert.")

Sometimes I also used "tickets out the door" or "exit slips"—the kids wrote one thing they learned that day and handed me their paper (the "ticket") at dismissal. If you've had a stressful day, end on a positive note by asking kids to share something they liked learning about or enjoyed doing in class.

Not only are these exit slips a fantastic assessment method and tool for discovering which activities are resonating with your students, but they're also a written record that *yes*, this day was worth getting out of bed for, because you did actually get through to some of the kids.

Stop by students' after-school activities and extracurriculars

This is an especially relevant suggestion for secondary teachers who have dozens of students and too little unstructured time in which to make personal connections. Make an effort once a week or so to swing by after-school band rehearsals, Yearbook Club meetings, and so on. Just say hi, observe the kids, and encourage them for a moment or two.

If you can attend school sports games, concerts, and other events, that's great, too. Sponsoring a club or coaching is even better! But even tutoring and extra credit study sessions are an opportunity to show kids that you care about them and are personally invested in their success.

Opportunities to connect with your students don't often happen naturally because the school day is just so busy. The more you choose to actively look for ways to acknowledge kids as individuals and enjoy their company, the more you will enjoy teaching them! Infuse your day with moments of connecting with students and building relationships, and you'll discover a new level of energy and enthusiasm for your work.

17

Choose to love kids most when they act most unlovable

Connecting and growing with your students is one of the most important ways to combat burnout and make teaching enjoyable. But if we're really honest, we'll admit that it's a lot harder to enjoy some kids than others.

Every class has at least a few students with defiant, disrespectful, anti-social, or just plain obnoxious behaviors. These particularly challenging kids can use up all your resolve so that you have nothing left to give the other students. And during those years that you have a classroom full of challenging behaviors, you might feel like quitting the profession altogether.

I'm going to share how you can make a conscious decision to fight against that discouragement, and decide: *I will love my students no matter what, even when they are acting unlovable.*

Here are some mindset shifts and practical tips to help you do that.

You can't control students' attitudes, but you CAN create the class climate

There were many years when I felt powerless over the type of day I had in the classroom. I would start off in a good mood, but a group of kids would come in arguing and shoving each other, and that would throw me off for the rest of the day. (*Oh, it's going to be one of those days, huh? I guess I can forget that new project I wanted to introduce — they can't handle it!*)

There were days when I had a lot of energy but the kids were reluctant to participate, and days when I was dragging but the kids were practically swinging from the ceiling. I felt like I never knew what to expect, and that I was at the mercy of whatever mood students were experiencing when they came to class.

I assumed I had no choice but to follow the kids' lead: if they were crazy, I resigned myself to a crazy day. But it was that resignation which derailed my plans. Rather than recognize my students' moods and steer the kids to a productive place, I allowed them to drain my energy and focus. I sacrificed my vision for the classroom because of a few eight-year-olds' bad attitudes!

Here's the conclusion that I finally learned the hard way: the teacher is always the most influential person in the room. It's true! The teacher is the deciding element.

That's why the same group of kids behaves completely differently when they have a substitute or go to P.E. or art. It's why one teacher can be reduced to tears by a group of students while another teacher creates order and commands respect from the same group within the first two minutes.

The teacher sets the behavioral norms, chooses the routines and plans the activities, and determines how to respond to students' off-task behaviors. The teacher creates the class climate.

Don't let kids' attitudes bring you down: choose to be the one who raises them up

We as teachers have the power to balance out kids' negative energy with our own positive energy. I won't sugar coat this: it's not always easy. When students are non-cooperative, you will have to put out a lot more energy than normal to shift the mood of the classroom. But it's something you *have* to do, no matter how hard it feels. For the sake of the kids as well as your own sanity, students' moods cannot be allowed to control your day.

You might not fully believe me when I say that you have the power to impact students' attitudes and energy levels. Here's the reasoning behind my statement: you have tremendous influence on how your students feel, and people act out of their feelings. If you help someone *feel* better, they will *behave* better.

Think about your relationship with your spouse or other members of your household. If you come home in a good mood but your spouse is irritable, it can bring you down. Conversely, if you're in a lousy mood but your spouse is empathetic, accommodating, and kind, you can bounce back more quickly.

Feelings are extremely contagious, and you can use that fact to your advantage. Create the positive energy when students don't bring it, and tone the energy down when students are overexcited. Use your kids' energy levels as a guide, but steer them the way you want. Play off their moods; if they're dragging, do some low-key activities, and if they're excited, do more active things. But never let them derail a lesson. You create the climate.

Don't take misbehavior as a personal attack

It's so frustrating when students talk back, call you names, and disrespect you. But it's easier to handle if you remind yourself that most of those actions are not really about you.

Not taking students' misbehavior personally has been a big struggle for me because I see my classroom as an extension of myself. I spend a tremendous amount of time creating a beautiful learning environment and designing engaging lessons, so when students don't follow the rules I set up or won't participate appropriately, I instinctively consider their actions as an attack on my system. I have often perceived kids' noncompliance as an affront to who I am as a teacher and as a person.

I have to consciously remind myself that children who are disrespectful, obnoxiously attention-seeking, or totally indifferent are not necessarily acting that way *toward me.* Kids act out in response to life situations and mental habits we can't begin to imagine. They rarely have a grasp on metacognition (the ability to think about their thinking) and have all sorts of thought processes that create extreme, unpredictable behaviors. How they feel about *you* and what they're being expected to do in the classroom is undoubtedly just one piece of the puzzle.

There are two approaches that have been helpful to me in learning not to take misbehavior personally. The first has been to create a more child-centered classroom and increasingly seek and value input from my students and their families. When I started to give the kids more ownership over their learning, I began to view the classroom as "our world" rather than "my world." This changed my perception so that students who didn't follow our rules were no longer challenging my authority; they just needed more support to be successful in meeting our agreed-upon class norms. As I relinquished control, I found that it was much easier to keep my peace and not take offense when dealing with defiant student behaviors.

Another approach that has been helpful in this area is being more pro-active in preventing behavior problems. I needed to spend more time identifying and addressing the reasons why children were acting out in the first place. Identifying kids' triggers often tells me a lot about why they are misbehaving, which means I can then put supports in place to prevent problems from occurring.

Off-task behavior vs. misbehavior

A lot of our frustration with kids stems from trying to pigeonhole them into the image of what we believe is the model student. We get angry when students aren't hanging on our every word or giddy with excitement over the assignments we give. Deep down, what most of us really want is for every single student to be at rapt attention during every single activity, every single day.

That's a great goal to strive for, but we can't allow discouragement to set in when it doesn't happen. The vast majority of the time, at least one student is going to fall short of our expectations. So we need to understand that we are creating our own stress and unhappiness by comparing reality to our ideal. We have to respond to disengaged and disruptive students calmly and not let them derail our enthusiasm for the lesson. If we allow every eye roll or deep sigh to send us off the rails, teaching is never going to be enjoyable.

Make sure you're not reacting to *off-task behavior* as if it is *misbehavior*. Sometimes there is nothing inherently wrong with the child's actions; it's only their timing that's inappropriate. Talking, playing, and being silly are perfectly appropriate behaviors for kids—just not in the middle of your instruction.

I can recall many times when I used the same tone and intensity in responding to students who whispered during a lesson as I did when students were about to get into a physical altercation! I really needed to take a deep breath and remind myself: *Off-task behavior, not misbehavior. I'm going to refocus the kids calmly, and not lose my peace over a few side conversations while I'm teaching.*

Stop the punishment cycle, and practice procedures

Here's a truly miserable way to spend your day: watch students like a hawk, looking for any evidence of misbehavior. Catch every incident, stop your lesson, and enforce a punishment. Monitor the child who's being punished while simultaneously watching for other rule breakers. Catch, punish, catch, punish. Repeat 7 hours a day, 5 days a week, 10 months a year.

Although I don't think any of us would describe our daily work in quite those terms, that's often the reality if we really take a hard look. We spend a tremendous amount of energy-draining time responding to misbehavior, and not enough time being proactive and setting kids up for success.

When students make poor choices, consider practicing procedures in place of punishment. Remember, kids have to not only learn your expectations; they have to *unlearn* those of their previous teachers, since everyone has different standards and routines. They also have to transition between the expectations for behavior at home, on the school bus, in the cafeteria, in their other teachers' classes, in after-school programs, and so on.

Imagine if you had 5 or 6 different bosses to report to at different times throughout the day and they each had a separate set of procedures, rules, and expectations. When you realize that's the situation your students are dealing with (and they are much less mature and self-aware than you are), then their need for constant reminders starts to make more sense. It's only natural that most students need several weeks to learn your expectations and will need continual reinforcement all the way through June.

Don't frustrate yourself by insisting, "They should know better by now!" You would think that by mid-year in the second or third (or twelfth!) grade, kids would automatically refrain from screaming in the hallway or cussing at each other when frustrated in class, but what we're asking them to do is often not part of their default, intuitive behaviors. We're asking kids to think carefully about their choices and make decisions that require a great deal of self-discipline. You can avoid losing your cool every time the kids act out by reminding yourself, *This is normal behavior for them, and needing more practice is normal! I can handle this!*

When a child makes the same mistakes or exhibits the same frustrating behaviors over and over again, break the punishment or yelling cycle with more opportunities for practice. If a student never remembers to turn in his assignment before leaving the classroom, don't yell or punish—simply say, "What needs to happen with your assignment? Thank you," or even just smile and point at the paper. Students often learn a lot more from practicing the right behavior than they do from being punished for the wrong behavior. Give them many, many opportunities to internalize your expectations.

During those times when you do need to give consequences, try to make sure they are related and logical, and enforce them in ways that are appropriate for individual children. For example, if a child is continually disruptive during group work, speak to her one-on-one to explain that she'll need to finish the assignment alone. Don't get drawn into an argument: repeat the consequence calmly and succinctly, then walk away.

Afterward, you must mentally move on with your day. Do not keep repeating the incident in your mind. Tell yourself, *I will not let the out-of-control emotions of a child create out-of-control emotions in me. I will act and not react. I will not carry this incident with me all day long. Once it's over, I'm letting it go.*

Meet students' unmet needs with love

Research has shown that there are 6 basic unmet needs that may cause a student to be disruptive and act out in class. A student might be acting out because she or he is: not clear about the expectations, wanting attention, bored, expelling excess energy, meeting a need for power or control, or trying desperately to avoid failure.

The key to solving behavior problems is to figure out which unmet need the child is attempting to address, and then help him or her meet that need. If a child is continually talking out of turn because she wants attention, your response should be different than if she's not clear on your expectation for hand raising, or if she's bored and wants to direct the conversation in another way. If a child is frequently disrespectful to a peer during group work, your reaction should depend on whether the motive was avoiding failure and looking dumb in front of his partner, or a need for control because the child gets frustrated when other kids' mistakes slow him down.

Each inappropriate behavior needs to be addressed. The reason is not an excuse. But your reaction should be based on the underlying issue. When you help kids figure out their own unmet needs and how to meet those needs productively, they feel better. And when kids feel better, they behave better.

Always make it your goal to respond in love. This is not so much about the type of correction but about the intention behind it. Love is something that permeates your heart attitude. When you correct or respond to a child from love, your intention is completely different than if you respond from anger, annoyance, or disapproval. Your intention shines through in your facial expression and tone. Your students will feel the genuine sense of caring and empathy behind your response, and they will respond in kind.

When you're not sure what a student's unmet need is, you might find it helpful to boil the problem down to a need for love, and then prompt yourself to meet *that* need. This response won't come naturally, for sure! But the children who need the most love often ask for it in the most unloving ways.

Think about your most difficult student. Can you see how she or he is desperate for the attention and approval of a loving, caring adult? Maybe the student is working below grade level and always feels stupid and left behind. Maybe the student is experiencing trauma at home. Maybe the student just never had anyone model appropriate social relationships and she or he can only think to resort to bullying, withdrawal, or anti-social behaviors.

Kids do not control *your* behaviors and emotions. You can choose to react to difficult students out of anger and spend most of your workweek in a rage, or you can choose to act from a place of love.

Fix your toughest behavior issues in 2 minutes a day

I've tried a lot of behavior management strategies throughout my career as a teacher and as an instructional coach, and I don't think I've ever used the term "miraculous" in relation to behavior management. But there is one strategy that might be as close as it gets, and it's a great example of meeting unmet needs from a place of love.

It's called the 2×10 strategy, and it's incredibly simple. Just spend 2 minutes per day for 10 days in a row talking with an at-risk student about anything she or he wants to talk about.

The approach is based on the research of Raymond Wlodkowski. His studies as well as those of other researchers have consistently found that the 2x10 Strategy not only creates an improvement in the targeted student's behavior, but typically improves the behavior of *all the other students in the class*, as well.

There's no mystery about why the 2x10 works, of course—it builds a rapport between teacher and student, and lets the child see that the teacher genuinely cares about him or her as a person. What makes this strategy seem miraculous is how it turns that abstract, overwhelming, where-do-I-start concept of relationship building into something easily manageable with an immediate payoff for everyone involved.

Considering how much time many of us spend addressing classroom disruptions and disciplining students, a 2-minute-a-day investment is an easy choice. I love that this strategy helps teachers focus on the good in their most challenging students so we can avoid falling into the trap of viewing a disruptive kid as a problem instead of a person. It's much easier to muster up the enthusiasm and patience you need for working with challenging kids if you have genuine empathy for them and get to spend time enjoying their company rather than always correcting them.

Recognize that behaviors and group dynamics WILL change

Discouragement can quickly set in when you assume you'll be dealing with the same set of behavior problems every day from now until June. But don't worry—that's definitely not going to happen.

Throughout the school year, you'll have new kids transfer into your class and others transfer out, shifting the dynamics of your group continually. The addition or subtraction of just one child can make a huge difference in how the whole class behaves and how you feel about your work.

Also, individual student behavior often changes a lot throughout the school year as students mature and as they experience shifts in their home and social lives. Some of the students who were the most difficult for me to handle in September ended up being a lot of fun to teach by the spring. Never lose faith in your students and assume they are incapable of change. They must sense that you believe in them and their potential to improve.

It's also important to prepare yourself for regression. Don't waste your energy moaning about how a child "used to be such a good student" and is now a huge pain all the time. Similarly, don't expect

100% consistency and get frustrated when a child has a bad day after a long string of good ones.

Though not all classroom changes are positive, take comfort in the fact that they *are* changes. You will not be dealing with the exact same problems from the exact same kids all day, every day for the entire year. A shift in your challenges could come at literally any minute. Stay focused on understanding and addressing kids' unmet needs, whatever they might be right now in this moment. Trust that setbacks are only temporary and that students will make positive progress over time.

You can handle ANY student behavior from now until June

It's very normal to have moments in the classroom in which you look around at all your challenging students and think, "I can't take this one more day; I have to quit teaching." But you must refuse to make any decisions about your job based on one year's class. Do not be swayed from a career path you once loved based on a single child or group of students you'll never have again.

Remember, this will all be over in June. Keep telling yourself, "I can do anything for a few more months." And when June comes, you'll get 6-9 weeks to recuperate and start fresh with a brand new class. Whatever issues you are facing with difficult personalities right now are only temporary–most people can't say that about their jobs.

Constantly telling yourself that you can't do this just adds to burnout. Instead, take steps to enjoy the kids you have right now in your classroom. Not the kids you wish you had, the kids you had last year, or the kids you hope to have next year. *These kids*, the ones who have been placed in your room for a purpose that is probably far greater than you will ever understand.

These students are *yours*: take them as they are, and love them through the unlovable parts. Your patience and compassion has the potential to influence them for a lifetime. The work you do with them each day matters. It molds them into the type of adult they will become. It shapes them for the future, and enables them to continue growing so they, too, can contribute great things to the world. Don't give up!

18

Be truly present and
look for the light bulb moments

Why is that you don't mind students calling your name for something off-topic at certain moments in a lesson, but at other times, you get annoyed and yell at kids for interrupting?

How come it's sometimes easy to respond patiently when students misbehave, and at other times, you feel like you can't deal with a certain behavior for *one more second* or you'll totally lose your mind?

Why do some directives or backhanded compliments from administration drive you up the wall, while you handle others with ease and grace?

The way we experience life's little (and big) annoyances is always filtered through our perception of them. That's good news, because it means that we are not powerless over how we feel. Much of our reaction to setbacks is related to how present we are in the moment and how we choose to perceive the obstacles in front of us. If you want to become more unshakeable, start focusing on being totally engaged in the moment.

The secret to patience is presence

Kids (and people in general) are the most annoying to us when they're interfering with other things we're trying to do which we think are more important. Anytime our current priority is completing a different task or we're someplace else mentally (such as trying to solve another problem), the person who is presently demanding our attention is going to feel like a stressor.

Imagine that your students keep coming over to ask you questions about a test you've already thoroughly and carefully explained. If you're simply circulating around the classroom and fully attending to the kids' needs—if you are completely present and your primary focus is on helping the class do well on the test—you will usually respond reasonably well to interruptions. You'll either answer the questions matter-of-factly, or will stop the class and calmly re-explain the directions. You might even have the presence of mind to inject some humor into the situation. It won't be the highlight of your day, but it also won't put you in a terrible mood and cause you to yell at your class.

However, if the kids are asking you the same questions over and over while you're trying to grade papers or fill out a behavior referral, your response probably won't be so patient.

Likewise, if they're asking you a million questions while you're mentally replaying the bad evaluation your principal just gave you, or you're on an internal tirade about how unfair it was that your planning time was just taken away...chances are good that you'll end up snapping at your students.

Each time you're pulled away from the physical or mental task you've decided is your most important focus right now, you're going to get more frustrated. You're then going to take that frustration out on your students and anyone else in your path, creating more negativity as well as guilt.

It is an endless downward cycle, and if you haven't formulated a game plan for decompressing, it will continue on through the next day, week, and month until you're completely exhausted and wonder how you grew to hate teaching. Yes, it's that serious.

How to respond to interruptions with patient presence

Sure, it would be great to have an important conversation with a colleague in the doorway while students continue working quietly, but the reality may be that a student is currently standing in front of you requesting assistance. Will you choose to accept that reality and focus your attention on him for a moment, or will you choose to hang onto your idea of what reality "should be", and get annoyed that he's interrupting you?

Similarly, if you're focused on covering those last two pages of the textbook, you have the choice to accept the reality that students' misbehavior is interfering with your lesson, or you can cling to your own idea of how the lesson is supposed to go and lose your temper because kids aren't paying attention.

Accepting reality doesn't mean allowing inappropriate behavior. It means being present with it, and turning your focus from what *you* want to accomplish to what your students really need from you right then. Meet *their* needs—acknowledge your students, redirect them, draw them back into the activity—and then turn your attention back to your lesson objectives.

When you're fully present with kids, you process interruptions and unwanted behaviors differently in your mind and attend to them rather than your own agenda. Choosing to be present will create a level of patience that softens your mood as well as your words, body language, and tone.

So how do you stay in the present moment? Choose your thoughts and focus on the task at hand. Stop thinking about things that already happened or worrying about the future or potential problems—remind yourself that you can think about that stuff later, if needed. Some of your problems or anticipated problems will go away on their own if you don't think about them, and the rest will still be there later. You really don't have to think about them right now, no matter how urgent they might seem!

Practice thinking only about the thing you're supposed to be doing right now. If you're feeling stressed, you must stop multi-tasking. Your brain is like a computer: it can only handle so many intensive tasks at one time, or it will freeze up and become worthless. Close out some of those other tasks that are draining your effectiveness and follow up with them later.

Attending to a class full of children is incredibly demanding just on its own. When you choose to be mentally and physically present with your students, you'll find it's infinitely easier to help them.

Let go of your attachment to The Plan so you can adapt to student needs

I'm the type of person who thinks through every task in advance and plans for the optimal way of completing it. I know exactly what time I need to set my morning alarm so I can get everything done. I know which route I want to drive to work so I can avoid the traffic lights. I have a routine when I first arrive in the school building that I feel confident is the most efficient and effective method.

The problem with planning everything out is that I am easily annoyed when things mess up my plans. And that's really not good when my plans for teaching are supposed to be about the kids. So, I've had to retrain myself to think of every plan I make as a simple guideline or outline that will be adjusted. In other words, I now *plan to be flexible* with my plan.

The end goal for a day of teaching can't be to "cover" a certain amount of curriculum; to cover means to obscure, and our goal is to illuminate. We must stay focused on illuminating the curriculum for students, and that can only be done by making a connection with them.

Anytime your focus is on finishing a project or "getting through" a page in the teachers' manual, you will become frustrated when outside circumstances prevent you from reaching your goal. A much more realistic and healthy goal is to be present with your students.

Don't wait for your administrators or school district to understand this: just do it. When you are focused on being tuned into kids, listening to kids, and responding to kids, *they will learn naturally*. Students will sense that they have your full attention and that you're enjoying interacting with them, and their engagement (and achievement) will increase as a result.

Full engagement is the greatest gift you can give your students (and yourself)

Total presence is becoming increasingly rare in our world. Young children are by nature fully immersed in whatever activity they're doing, but even that is changing as early technology use impacts their attention span and focus. Now more than ever, having someone's total time and energy feels like a special privilege...and yet it should be the norm.

I used to have an acquaintance who was never really present with me when we spent time together. She checked her phone constantly during our conversations. When I was speaking, she often looked past me to see who else was entering the room, or gazed off somewhere in a way that made it clear her mind was on something else. She always left our get-togethers early because she booked another obligation immediately afterwards. Spending time with her made me feel insignificant, and I wondered why she continued to initiate contact when her actions showed she really didn't value my company.

Conversely, I have a very dear friend who listens intently to every word I say to her. She looks me in the eye when I'm speaking. She's observant and notices when my body language contradicts what I'm saying. If her husband or children need her attention during our conversations, she says excuse me before attending to them and apologizes afterward, making sure to return to the exact point I was making before the interruption. She has a beautiful way of making every person she interacts with feel like they are the only person in the world at that moment, and that makes her attention feel like a gift and a privilege.

It's no mystery which person I chose to keep in my life and grow closer to.

Having someone's time *and* energy, their full presence in both body *and* mind—is one of the most precious things you can offer to your students and other people you care about. When you give not just your time but also your energy to the people around you, you will experience moments of full engagement. This is sometimes called flow: your sense of time passing just slips away because you are totally immersed in the present moment.

Those moments of flow and total engagement are the most rewarding ones you will ever experience in life. Your most enjoyable moments are never the ones in which you are splitting your energy between two different tasks simultaneously. Full engagement and full presence will make teaching more enjoyable for you and more meaningful for your students.

Do you smile while you're teaching?

This was a question I first considered when I took a classroom management course in college, and it had a huge impact on what would become my natural teaching style. What's remarkable is that the professor didn't tell us to smile: *she just did it* during her own instruction, and that demeanor made a permanent impression on me.

The professor didn't wear a fake or cheesy grin as she taught; she just let her natural love for the subject matter shine through. She told stories from her personal experiences a lot, and those made her smile. She quipped jokes—more smiles. And when she asked a question and paused for us to think and raise our hands, she smiled expectantly, as if she was anticipating such wonderful answers from her students that she couldn't wait to see what we'd share next.

That ever-present smile made learning so enjoyable. I felt like she genuinely liked me as a student, and that she liked her job. I started to notice the difference in my motivation level when the professors in other classes didn't smile unless something was really funny. I started to practice smiling during my student teaching experiences until it became a habit...and now I smile when I teach, too.

Here's the message that smiling at students communicates to them: *I'm here, right now, with you. I'm paying attention to you. I'm interested in you.* A person with a blank or neutral expression could be hiding any emotion or be a million miles away mentally. But it's nearly impossible to smile genuinely at someone if you are concentrating on something other than them. So if you want to try being more present with your students, just smile at them, and presence will naturally follow.

Try sharing a fact with the class and then say, "So, what do you think? Anyone have some ideas on that?" and smile expectantly during a few seconds of wait time. Project the energy to your class that you believe they are going to say something highly intelligent or thoughtful in response. I think you'll notice immediately that some of your hesitant students feel more comfortable participating when they see a warm, welcoming smile that communicates, *You have something important to say and I want to hear it.*

There's an added bonus for you as the teacher: smiling creates positive feelings, even when you're not feeling particularly happy. Numerous studies have found that choosing to smile can relieve stress and induce feelings of happiness. Feelings often follow action, so choose to behave the way you want to feel.

Stay present in mundane and hectic moments by finding something worth savoring

Part of the reason why we're not always present with our students in the classroom is that we're incredibly busy. We don't feel like we have a moment to savor *anything* even if we wanted to.

Compounding the problem is the fact that a lot of our work is not really fun. Who wants to be fully present in a moment that requires you to reprimand a child for not doing homework? How do you savor the moment when the moment involves scraping gum off a desk or filling out forms or quieting down an overly energetic class after lunch?

One of the ways to be present through the less enjoyable and even hectic aspects of our work is to be intentional about how we use that time. We can choose to incorporate ways of thinking and acting that make the time feel special or even sacred.

Do I sound crazy to admit that when I'm making photocopies, I revel in the chance to stand there quietly without any little voices calling my name? The sound of the machine humming is soothing. I like to feel the warmth of the paper as I pull the freshly run copies out of the tray.

I can just stand there and breathe, clearing my mind of everything except the next page I need to run through the machine. I can also use the time to think about how I'm going to use the copies, and the way I want to implement my lessons. Though I can't say I look forward to it, I am able to be intentional about how I use my time at the copier, and this routine makes the task a little more pleasurable.

When I line students up for lunch, I try to observe them carefully. Not to make sure they're doing the right thing, though that's always a temptation. Instead of looking for off-task behavior, I try to look at the *people* who are standing in front of me.

The kids are usually excited and looking forward to a time to chat with their friends, so they're smiling and enthusiastic. It's hard to look at someone else smiling and not smile yourself, so I welcome every grin. I pay attention to the way the afternoon sunlight is starting to filter through the windows, and I take a deep breath, satisfied that we've accomplished a lot that morning and the upcoming lunch break is well-deserved.

All of this happens in just two or three seconds, right before I turn off the lights and lead my class quietly down the hall. It's a short moment of true presence.

These habits don't come naturally to me. The day of a teacher is nonstop. If I'm not conscious about practicing presence, I'll spend the time at the photocopier seething that I have to run off so many pointless worksheets for test prep, and use the lining up time to nag my students to hurry as I anxiously watch the clock. I have to *practice* being present in the moment, and create productive habits that make hectic and mundane moments feel worth savoring.

Celebrate your small moments of accomplishment

Every day of being a teacher is filled with moments of potential joy and satisfaction. I use the word "potential," because you have to pay close attention and really be present if you want to grab onto those small, beautiful moments. There were many, many days when I was distracted and completely missed them because I was in such a hurry to *get to the next thing.* I never took time to stop mentally for even a second and revel in what my students and I had achieved.

Train your brain to find and dwell on those moments of accomplishment. Don't mentally replay the moment when a student disrespected you or a colleague was condescending: return your mind to the instant when you finally entered all that data into the computer, or cleared out your email inbox, or finished the lesson plans for the week.

You worked hard for those accomplishments! Don't skip over them and hurry on to the next item on your to-do list. Celebrate yourself. Give yourself the encouragement and praise you would give a student: *Yes, you did it! You're on fire today. Look how much you got done! You didn't want to do that task, but you pushed through it, anyway. Good job.*

Look for the light bulb moments and focus on a child you can really help

The obvious highlight of any teacher's day is the moment when information clicks for students and they really, truly *get it*. Those are the fleeting moments that you need to hold onto more than any other, because they remind you of your passion for teaching, your vision for the classroom, and the reason why you get up every morning and give so much of yourself to your students. Don't let those moments slip away!

Introduce the term "light bulb moment" or "aha moment" to your students and tell the kids how much you enjoy watching them learn new things. When you see the light bulb go off for a child, draw attention to it. Celebrate their persistence as well as their accomplishment. Write the "aha" down, either privately or in a public space in your classroom where kids can record big understandings and breakthroughs.

As you do these things, stay in the present moment. Don't let the joy of watching kids learn get muddled by the off-task behavior of another child nearby. Redirect as needed, but keep your thoughts centered on the good stuff that's happening right in front of you.

When you leave school at the end of the day, think back on those light bulb moments. Treasure them and use them to inspire you to go back into the classroom the next day and give it your all once again. Don't mentally replay the incidents when a kid totally disrupted your entire day. Choose to focus on the students you made a difference for.

If there is even *one* child in your class who cared about what you taught and made an effort to learn it, you have done something worthwhile. Use that student to motivate you to get up in the morning. Look over at him or her when you start to feel discouraged during a lesson. Press on toward more light bulb moments with that child and everyone else.

Reframe your work to recognize and appreciate the magnitude of what you do

When you are truly present in the classroom, you will start noticing all the small wins and celebrating the light bulb moments. You'll find yourself getting back in touch with the reason why you entered this profession in the first place. You'll start to realize what a tremendously important job you are doing every single minute of the day.

And then you'll be able to reframe how you view your work.

Do you think you spent the last 15 minutes tying shoes and zipping coats? No, you smiled at each of your students as you bundled them up to protect them from the cold. That might be the most loving, nurturing gesture some of those kids got all day.

Do you think you just wasted an entire afternoon in a data chat meeting? No, you got to step back and look at all the hard work you did compiling and analyzing information over the past week. You got to see all the evidence of just how well you really know your students, and you got to learn even more information that is going to empower you to take your kids to the next level tomorrow. Who cares if your principal's attitude made the meeting miserable? Look at what *you* did! Look how ready you are to meet your students' needs because of *your* hard work! Don't let anyone take that away from you!

Do you think you just taught a developmentally inappropriate learning standard that less than half the class truly understood? No, you helped 12 kids meet an incredibly difficult objective. 12 different kids, all at the same time! And you planted a seed for another dozen kids who are now a few steps closer to understanding the concept when you re-teach tomorrow.

This is not overly optimistic thinking—this is realistic thinking. It's reality. This is exactly what you did.

You *show up*, day after day, and work these little miracles all day long without even realizing you're doing it. You're probably so focused on everything you *didn't* do that you don't realize how much you've actually accomplished. I am urging you—stop for a moment. Be present. See what you are doing. Really, truly, *see it*.

Your work is important. Ultimately, whether someone else tells you that or not is irrelevant. You must choose to perceive your own work as something meaningful and valuable, because *it is*. Be present in every moment of it. It all matters, and it's all worth it.

19

Re-write the story
you tell yourself about teaching

You're finishing this book with lots of tools for living a more balanced life and finding more joy in teaching. You've learned how to use your time wisely, gain energy from the kids you teach, and do your part to build a positive school culture.

So, you know the *actions* you want to take. But you can't just plug the ideas from this book into a negative story that you're living out. The story you tell yourself is how you experience life, and you have to line up your mindset for the changes to stick. This is why most New Years resolutions don't work: people choose new actions, but keep telling themselves the same old stories. The old mindset does not support the new habits, and the mindset is far more powerful.

If you keep telling yourself that your job is too demanding and you'll never be able to keep up with it all, that will continue to be the story of your life, and the attempts you make to change won't last very long.

If you keep telling yourself it's impossible to have any time or energy for your own kids and family, that is the story you are destined to live. You might try to implement some of the family-first ideas I've shared, but your mindset will keep pulling you back to that same story and old patterns of behavior.

Here's the good news: you can re-write those stories about how you are helpless and powerless, and start telling yourself that you can change things that are not working in your life. You can write an empowering story that you will enjoy living.

For each new story you write, you can choose a new habit, as well. This habit will reinforce your new story and help make it a reality. Over time, you can add more habits to support your new story and create the life you want to live.

What is the story you're telling yourself about teaching?

Your story is the way you choose to interpret the events that happen in your life. Think of it as a framework for making meaning from the things that happen to you. The human brain is wired to create meaning and tell stories. It makes connections between events and draws conclusions about them automatically, often without us even realizing it.

Most of us have many stories that overlap and sometimes even contradict one another. We repeat these stories to ourselves over and over so that they become a subconscious part of our thought process. Some stories are productive and helpful, while others are confining and prevent us from seeing new possibilities.

If you have a negative story about teaching, then any time a problem or conflict arises, your story will be strengthened: "See, this is what I always say! The whole profession is going down the drain!" or "Here we go again, it's just one more thing piled onto my plate. I knew this was going to happen!"

Your stories become your script for living. You cannot easily deviate from a story because it's so ingrained in your thinking patterns. Your story shows through in everything about you, from your posture to your countenance. It impacts your energy level, your relationships, and even your physical health.

If you're not happy in teaching, you've probably been telling yourself a negative story and then living that story out, day after day after day. Your story might sound something like this:

This job is killing me. It gets worse every year! We have zero control over what and how we teach. No one respects us as professionals. The parents think they know more than we do and blame us for everything. The kids keep getting lazier and more disrespectful. The politicians run the school system and they're all idiots. There's just nothing fun about teaching anymore. I'm underpaid and overworked. It's impossible to enjoy this job.

As you read this, you might be thinking, "Yep, tell me about it. Story of my life." And that's what I want to help you change.

How are you justifying your negative stories about teaching?

Listen to the way you talk about your profession. Pay attention to the stories you tell other people about your day, and the way you frame events that happen. What occurrences cause a knee-jerk stress reaction in you? Notice your own mental habits, your self-talk, and the way you internally process the day's events and your life as a whole.

Ask yourself: *Is the story I'm currently telling myself about teaching producing the results I want? And if it's not, what's the story I'm telling myself to justify it?*

For instance, you might be telling yourself the story that no one respects the work you do. Does that story produce anything positive in your life? Chances are good that it's just depressing you. So what are you telling yourself to justify keeping that bad story around?

Why are you choosing to tell yourself something so defeating, and then live that story out?

That story is not the whole truth. There *are* people who respect the work you do. *You* respect the work you do. Maybe you keep repeating that story because it allows you to feel sorry for yourself. Maybe it earns you sympathy from someone. Maybe it's an attempt to get more respect and draw attention to your plight as a teacher. Or maybe you just feel helpless and don't know what else to tell yourself.

If the story is not producing the results you want—peace, fulfillment, enthusiasm, and happiness—*you cannot keep telling it*. If you do, you will continue a vicious cycle: tell the story, live it out, tell the story, live it out.

You'll never go above and beyond for your school community because your story insists your efforts won't be appreciated, anyway. You'll feel miserable dragging your work home in the evenings because the story running through your mind says students and families don't care or respect your time. In this way, you become stuck in miserable thought and behavior patterns that continually reinforce one another.

It's time to break the cycle. It's time for a re-write. You can flip the script and compose a new teaching story.

What is the story that will produce the results you want in life?

You must identify any story about teaching that is making you unhappy, and then write the story you want to live. Write the story that is true to your values and what you believe is most important. Write the story that inspires you to go into the classroom every day and give your all.

If your story is similar to the example I gave on the previous page ("this job is killing me"), your rewrite might sound something like this:

I am grateful for my job. I spent years preparing for this teaching position and interviewing for it, and I am going to enjoy it, no matter what. My students are my greatest teachers. Interacting with them and learning how to meet their needs makes me a better person. I give 100% of myself to building relationships with my students' parents and choose to view them as my allies and partners, regardless of how they respond to me.

I have the power to make a difference for my students in any circumstance, amidst any bureaucracy. I find and take every opportunity I can get to enjoy teaching and have fun helping my students learn. I make time for myself and the things and people that matter most to me. I am unshakeable in my enthusiasm for this job.

Note that this story is grounded in the same reality and facts as the original story. It's just interpreted differently. It's written in a way to produce feelings of empowerment rather than discouragement. It's designed to let go of old, unproductive ideas about teaching and replace them with the mindset that you are completely capable of thriving in any situation.

You might not fully believe this new story yet. That's okay. Start telling it to yourself anyway, because *this story is the kind of story you want to live.* This story will produce the results you want, and when you combine it with new habits, it will become a reality.

How to use ideas from this book to create new stories & habits

Start by figuring out which stories are wreaking the most havoc in your life. You might want to choose the single most detrimental story to begin with. Then, go back to the relevant chapter(s) in this book and look for ideas you highlighted. Which practices resonated most with you? Use those ideas to write your new story out and choose your new habits.

Your new story could be a single sentence to start with, and can be paired with just one habit that reinforces it. Every day, read and repeat your new story to yourself as many times as possible, and put the habit into practice.

Here are some examples of stories you might currently be telling yourself, along with a new story and habit to change it:

I can't have fun with my students because there's no time for it.
New story: I create daily routines that make learning fun for me and my students.
New habit: Use the 30 second dance party to celebrate kids' work.

My students' parents make my job miserable.
New story: I choose to view parents as my partners.
New habit: I will hold a Family Festivity one time per month to build a rapport with parents.

My district makes it impossible for me to teach the way I want to.
New story: I choose to exercise my freedom and creativity every chance I get.
New habit: Find one fun new teaching strategy for each unit I teach.

I can't feel good about myself when I'm being evaluated unfairly.
New story: I know my own worth and define success for myself.
New habit: Repeat my vision every day before and after work.

I can't keep a good attitude because I'm surrounded by negativity.
New story: I choose to seek out people who inspire and uplift me.
New habit: Join a Facebook group for positive teachers who enjoy sharing ideas.

I can never achieve a work-life balance.
New story: I manage my time and energy well, and create effective schedules.
New habit: Schedule time in the evening for family first, and use the leftover time for work.

I can't do a good job because I don't have the necessary materials.

New story: I am creative and resourceful about meeting my students' needs.

New habit: I will spend one hour a week looking for great teaching resources online.

I don't have time for getting the sleep I need.

New story: I make time for sleep because I know it creates more energy the next day.

New habit: Go to bed at 11 pm every night, regardless of what's done or not done.

I don't have time to stop multi-tasking and just be present.

New story: The best gift I can give to people around me is to be fully engaged with them.

New habit: Turn my phone off during instructional hours and between 7 and 10 pm.

I can't enjoy teaching standards that are too hard for my students.

New story: I can uncover a compelling reason for every standard I teach and make it meaningful for my students.

New habit: Post "why" on my board before each lesson and help kids make connections to how the skill is relevant to their lives.

There's no way I can enjoy teaching with THAT kid in my class.

New story: I create the classroom climate. I choose to bring kids up rather than letting them bring me down.

New habit: Implement the 2x10 strategy with my most challenging student.

Every time you find yourself thinking along the lines of your old story, stop and replace it with the new one. Repeat the story you want to live and practice the new habit with intention on a daily basis. This will retrain your mind to internalize the new story and make it a natural part of your life in a surprisingly short amount of time.

Stack up your productive "new story" habits

Once you successfully put your new habit in place and your new story starts to become your default thought pattern, you will realize just how simple the process of re-writing your teaching story can be. Your initial success will give you confidence in the process and yourself. The new story will start popping into your head automatically and you will see more opportunities for habits that support that story.

When you feel ready, stack another habit on top of the old one. For example, if your new story is that you can thrive as a teacher no matter what kind of leadership your principal provides, your first new habit might be related to taking charge of your own professional development. You might choose to learn about a topic that you're interested in, despite a lack of support from your principal.

Once you've successfully created that habit, keep repeating the new story about thriving no matter what, and stack another habit on top, perhaps finding a mentor for yourself so that you can hear positive and constructive feedback on your teaching. Later, you might add a habit of meeting with your grade level team once a week during lunch to share what's working. These habits, once accumulated, bring your new story to reality.

You can also begin tackling more stories. Maybe your other big problem is that you've convinced yourself you'll never be able to find the time, energy, or money to do things you enjoy. So, write your new story: *I make time for the things that matter most to me, and I am a priority in my own life.*

Create and implement one habit related to the new story, such as reading something you enjoy from 10:15-10:30 pm every night. Then stack another habit on top: going out for happy hour with friends one time a month. Stack another habit on top of that: going to a yoga class two times a week, or joining a club centered around that hobby you've always wanted to pursue.

Before you know it—often within only a week or two--you will find yourself beginning to live out your new story. As you stack more habits, you will start to see major changes in your energy level, productivity, and satisfaction with work and life in general. Your new, positive story will become part of your natural way of thinking, and your new habits will ensure that your lifestyle is aligned with that.

20

Innovate and adapt to make teaching an adventure

As you reach the end of this book, my hope is that you're feeling inspired and have a lot of new ideas to take into the classroom. You might already be thinking about other books and resources you can tap into, or how to connect with inspiring educators online. Surrounding yourself with these encouraging resources will keep you pumped up and feeling ready for anything that comes your way in teaching.

But when you step back into your classroom again, you may find that reality comes crashing down on you. The demands of the job might start to feel frustrating, or you might feel discouraged and overwhelmed when another new problem crops up. Everything you learned and everything that motivated you might go right out the window as you slip back into survival mode and those same old habits.

Here's what I want you to do when any of that stuff happens. *I want you to think of teaching as an adventure.*

What's the first thought that comes to mind when you hear the word "adventure"? Maybe you think of skydiving, or exploring a new city you've never been to before. Maybe an adventure to you is showing up to an outlet mall with $500. Regardless of your choice, I think it's a fair assumption that most of us don't think of anything related to work.

I've found that the secret to making teaching feel like an adventure is reflecting on and creating new challenges, making peace with the unknown, and embracing change even at the risk of failure. Let's break each one of those aspects down individually.

Reflect on what's working, what's not, and why

Most of us are too busy to regularly—or ever—step back from our daily routines and reflect on what is and isn't working. But researchers have found time and again that personal reflection is one of the most important keys to effective teaching. I think that's particularly true considering how many new situations and challenges we have to adapt to on a regular basis. What worked with the old standards might not work with the new, and what was effective with kids last year might not be what your class needs this year.

You know the old saying, "Those who don't know history are doomed to repeat it"? That's true in our personal and professional lives, as well. If you just keep plodding along without taking the time to understand your successes and failures, you won't really know what created them, and therefore you won't know which practices you should keep and which to let go of.

See if you can create a habit of reflecting on your work for just a few minutes each day. Ask yourself,

What was the best part of this day?
What did I do to create or contribute to that success?
What was something I'd like to see go better next time?

How did I contribute to that obstacle or setback?
What can I do to improve?
What is the biggest lesson I learned today?
What am I most looking forward to tomorrow?

Try to make clear connections between your thoughts/actions and what worked or did not work. Don't blame shift, as you can only control your *own* actions. Don't obsess over your shortcomings, either—failure is a critical part of the learning process. Stay focused on what you can learn from your own choices and mistakes.

I've also found it very helpful to reflect in writing on my lessons, especially during school years in which I experienced a lot of changes and unknowns, such as a new grade level or curriculum. I didn't comment on every lesson I taught, but tried to record reflections that I thought were important for future lesson planning.

When I kept a paper lesson plan book, I'd grab a sticky note and jot down very quick reminders to myself whenever I had a minute: *Kids were totally lost with this: next time try ___* or *This activity worked so much better halfway through the lesson when I finally ___*. Later on when I kept my lessons digitally, I created a box in my daily grid especially for typing in reflections.

These notes not only helped me solidify my reflections on teaching and create a game plan for the next day's lessons, they also helped me avoid making the same mistakes the following year. I'd read over my previous year's notes when I wrote new lesson plans, and it felt like having the inside scoop or a behind-the-scenes glance at what works in the classroom. I couldn't believe how many great strategies I'd forgotten I'd tried and all the little tweaks I'd learned along the way.

I also took a few minutes to write a reflection at the end of each unit and each school year. Sometimes I wrote more detailed reflections and shared them on my blog, and my most profound reflections usually came from that process. It's amazing how many times I didn't know what I really thought or felt about a teaching practice until I tried to convey everything in writing.

I know many, many teachers who author small (often password-protected) blogs just to reflect on their own practice, and I highly encourage you to consider that option. It's incredibly insightful to look back over the years and see how much your thinking and teaching has changed.

Whatever methods you choose, developing a practice of reflection will help you feel more confident about taking risks and enable you to see patterns in what works and what doesn't. When you're faced with yet another change or unexpected event, you will be less likely to force your old way of doing things into a new situation just by default.

Reflecting will give you the confidence and the action research needed to come up new ideas that will work even better. When you believe in your own ability to identify what works and problem-solve around what doesn't, you will be better equipped to withstand any new mandate that comes your way.

Prevent burnout by choosing your own change and challenges

The concept of purposely seeking out change can seem like an odd solution in a field where things never stay the same for long, especially since most people think they don't like change. But if you consider the issue a little more deeply, you'll probably realize that you enjoy or even thrive off of change that you initiate and design yourself (as opposed to change that is thrust upon you without your input.)

Every teacher I've talked to who really loves his or her job has cited professional change as one of the main ways they've prevented burnout. When happy teachers start to lose their enthusiasm, they switch grade levels or schools. They take on a different extracurricular role or committee responsibility. They request to teach advanced placement classes, find a way to co-teach, work as a Title I teacher in small group settings, shadow an administrator and take leadership courses, or get a special education or gifted endorsement. Every teaching position is incredibly unique, and you'd be amazed at how a role with a better fit for your changing personality and needs can completely transform your experience of being an educator.

Even if you don't (or can't) change your teaching position, you can create a self-directed challenge that reflects who you are and who you want to become professionally in order to feel more motivated at work.

I like to create a challenge for myself in one major area during each school year. I developed monthly parent workshops one year and planned ways to strengthen my communication and relationships with families. Another year, I read every book I could find on Writer's Workshop and developed a huge repertoire of best practices for writing instruction. Another year, I created backward planning units for science to make sure I was teaching kids the big ideas and essential questions.

Choosing new ideas to try out made teaching feel fresh and exciting during times when I was bored by the status quo and felt powerless to change many other aspects of my job. It was invigorating to pursue ideas I was interested in, and it made teaching feel more like an adventure that I could look forward to.

Become a risk-taker who can embrace the unknown

By very definition, an adventure involves risk and an uncertain outcome. That's what makes adventures so exciting and fun! The unknown is what gets your heart pounding with anticipation. It keeps you fully present and fully engaged. It's not really an adventure if you know exactly what will happen next and you allow your mind to wander elsewhere.

So if your work in the classroom starts to feel monotonous or unrewarding, it could mean that you are not approaching teaching as an adventure. You are not staying fully engaged (giving all your time *and* energy in the present moment) and taking risks. You may find yourself feeling overwhelmed by all the variables you cannot control, and that makes you feel too tired or afraid to step out and try something new. You end up doing the same thing the same way and settling for the same familiar outcome.

The unknown is a scary thing for many people, and that's very understandable. There are certainly a lot of unknowns in education that create anxiety: Will you have the same teaching assignment next year? Will you even have a job? Will you get a pay raise or a pay freeze? What if the school district adopts a different textbook series? What if you get a new student who completely destroys the wonderful classroom community you've created?

But please hear me on this: you will never be happy as long as you insist on knowing what's going to happen in the future.

There will always be something to worry over or try to figure out. So, you can spend time mulling over every possible situation and outcome, or you can choose to trust that you'll be able to handle whatever comes your way.

Trusting yourself to be able to deal with anything will help you focus your energy on making peace with the unknown instead of trying to control it. Believe that things will ultimately work together for your good. You are resilient!

Even though you don't know right now what will happen or how you'll respond in the future, trust that you *will* know. Keep your focus on what's happening in the present moment, and stay fully engaged in the adventure you're experiencing now.

Run toward the changes in education so you don't get run over

Being comfortable with the unknown is a critical mindset to adapt in teaching because the policy pendulum is continually swinging from one end of the spectrum to the other. New standards, curriculum, technology, and initiatives seem to present themselves almost overnight, and it can feel impossible to keep up with the constant changes. However, you can choose to perceive this as part of the adventure, too.

If a change or new initiative has the potential to be good for your students, don't fight it. Instead, jump into problem-solving mode as soon as possible: *How can I incorporate this change into what I already know is effective for me and my students? What can I do to make this change work to my advantage?* Accept that you will be uncomfortable for a little while, but believe in your heart that the new changes will not undo you.

Dig in your heels and remember: you were there before the new initiative, and you will be there after it's gone. Policies and educational trends come and go, but you have the perseverance to outlast them all. Envision yourself as a tree by the river, firmly planted, swaying as the winds and rain come, but never uprooted.

And when faced with systemic changes that are clearly bad for kids and teachers, your ultimate goal must be to maintain your enthusiasm for teaching. Complaining all day and obsessing all night does nothing to help you or the kids. It only creates burnout, and a burned out, jaded teacher is of no value to anyone.

You can work to create a positive influence on the system whenever possible. I deeply respect teachers who join online and local groups that push to create change and make teachers' voices heard. When you are passionate about making a difference, it's a good thing to spend some of your time fighting for what's right.

But there is a huge difference between speaking truth to power and complaining; between advocacy and preaching to the choir. When you take on the gigantic task of fighting policies, systems, and governments, you must participate in productive activities that further your cause, and then turn your mind and heart back to your daily work with students. Don't lose sight of the tremendous impact you have on education at a grassroots level, making a difference for one child at a time through your classroom choices.

For the sake of your students, you must keep a resolute, focused mindset while at school: *I will not frustrate myself by trying to control things I cannot control. I accept that sometimes things are unfair and do not make sense. I refuse to lose my peace over something inane. No setback can stop me from being a good teacher. I will push through the bureaucracy and the learning curve and I will be successful for the sake of my students, no matter what.*

Don't just stand still and brace for impact. Run toward the changes in education. Be an innovator. Be the one who looks at a difficult situation and figures out how to make the changes work to your benefit and the kids'.

Choose to innovate and subvert the system quietly

You cannot create additional pressure for yourself by constantly thinking about how high the stakes are. If you obsess over producing excellent test scores and getting stellar evaluations, the fear of making a mistake can become paralyzing. You'll end up convincing yourself that you cannot deviate from The Plan, express any creativity, or try any unproven ideas. Teaching and learning then become a robotic, passionless experience for everyone in the classroom. The adventure is completely lost.

Now, it's true that innovation is not often rewarded in schools. There is great risk and little reward for sticking your neck out and being the one to try something different. I know this. And I'm encouraging you to do it, anyway.

Why? Because this is *your* job. More importantly, *this is your life.* Viewing yourself as a victim of bureaucracy is disempowering. No one should waste his or her life with that mindset. You have tremendous power and value as a teacher which you must hold onto, no matter who challenges you or how. Teachers are some of the most resilient, determined people in the world—look at how many obstacles we face and overcome on a daily basis!

You do not have to give away all your power to a broken system. You're a professional and you have the right to assert some control over how you teach. You don't have to simply do as you're told when what you're being told is wrong.

Throughout history, many lives have been lost due to those in lower areas of authority saying they were just following orders, and many of our students' lives are being destroyed by the same line of reasoning. We do not have to stand by and watch our children's love of learning be crushed by a system that is not designed to support them.

When you are told to do something that is clearly a waste of your time and does not benefit your students in any way, resist the urge to complain or fall into a passive "I don't have a choice" mindset. Ask yourself, *What would I do to subvert this directive if my or my students' lives depended on it?* Because in a way, your vitality and that of your students is in fact at stake. Ask yourself, *What happens if I don't?*

I assure you that the best teachers I know are quietly subverting the system in this way. You'd never know they're doing it, and that's the point. They're not trying to make a bold statement; they're just trying to do what's best for kids. They go through the motions (or appear to be doing so), but never let pointless policies interfere with what their kids need.

You have to trust your own judgment even when those in positions of authority don't empower you to do so. Hold tight to every opportunity you have to express your creativity in the classroom. You can't loudly refuse every mandate that comes down the pike. Be quietly subversive sometimes. Grab every single chance you get to close your door and do what's best for kids.

Never make instructional decisions based on fear

I once transferred to a school that had purchased three different math workbooks for its third grade students. My team leader informed me that the kids were supposed to complete every single page in all three workbooks by the end of the school year.

I blinked. "Wait...so the kids have to do 3 pages of nearly identical worksheets for every single lesson I teach in math?"

"Yep," my team leader said, matter-of-factly.

"But...why?"

"Because the school spent a lot of money on them and the principal doesn't want anything to go to waste."

"So...what if the kids *don't* do every page? Will I get in trouble?"

"You could, yeah. The assistant principal has been known to flip through the workbooks to make sure they're done. You're new here; I wouldn't rock the boat. Just have the kids do one page in class at the end of the lesson, one page for homework, and the other page the next morning as a warm up."

There was absolutely no way I was going to subject my kids to filling out three workbook pages a day in a single subject (on top of weekly benchmark assessment tests and bi-weekly unit tests.) Each workbook page took the kids 20-45 minutes. How would I have time to teach?

So, I used the pages that I thought were most relevant and skipped the rest. I did not tell anyone I was doing this: I didn't want a reputation for being rebellious or uncooperative, and I didn't need the rumor mill cranking up. I just taught the way I knew was best for my kids, and I had a ready defense of my practice in mind in case anyone ever asked.

My administrators did indeed flip through my workbooks one day that December. They wanted to see a particular student's work for a standard he hadn't mastered on a recent benchmark test. I showed them the workbook pages the student had done, the hands-on activities he'd completed, the data from a math partner game he'd played every day for the past two weeks, and a higher-level thinking project the student had worked on throughout the month.

The assistant principal was incredibly impressed by the rigor of my activities and wide variety of artifacts, and never even seemed to notice that the workbook was half empty. He knew I was a good teacher, and was well aware from his frequent walk-through observations that I was pushing my students hard every day. I also had plenty of documentation to back up my instructional choices, and I was armed with research to support my teaching methodology if anyone had questioned it.

But they didn't question it. No one ever looked at my workbooks again for the rest of the year. And no one ever looked at my colleagues' workbooks at *any* point during the year.

In June, I found out that another one of my team members had quietly subverted the system just as I had. But two of the other third grade teachers had dutifully forced their students to complete three workbook pages a day in math, often in addition to textbook work, simply because *they were afraid of getting caught doing the right thing by their students.*

It sickens me to think about my colleagues feeling pressured to do something every day that they and their students resented. How many hundreds of hours did those teachers waste grading three pages when one would have been plenty to tell them if kids had mastered the concept? And even worse, how many hundreds of hours did the students waste on unnecessary practice, squandering an opportunity to learn in a real world context and solve problems that actually matter? Who knows how many of those children were turned off to math or learning in general because school leaders had created fear in the hearts of their teachers.

You cannot make instructional decisions based on fear. You must be motivated by what is best practice and most effective for kids. You must be quietly subversive, picking your battles carefully and humbly making sound choices. You do not have to be a pawn, perpetuating an unfair game that you and your students are destined to lose.

Don't internalize the external pressure

It's almost comical how the directives we're given as teachers seem to be framed as life or death situations that must be addressed immediately:

Remember that system for data collection you spent the entire second semester learning last year? Yeah, we're not doing things that way anymore. Learn a new system! The training is this Thursday from 3-5 pm; too bad if you had other obligations. And here's a new math curriculum, too—that needs to be implemented before the end of the week. We have to improve our scores! More data! More testing! More accountability! And it all has to happen perfectly starting on day one!

Don't internalize this pressure, my friends. Be kind to yourself. The weight that a classroom teacher carries is heavy enough on its own. Don't add to it by buying into the myth that you must be a super teacher, performing miracles at every turn, compelling all students to work on or above grade level simply through the sheer amount of energy and time that you expend.

What you do *is* miraculous, but it's not always measurable. And it doesn't have to be. You're getting a student to open up about the hard times he's having at home. You're supporting a child who doesn't speak English as she makes new friends. You're instilling a love of learning in a student who hates school. You're moving your class toward skill mastery in small, uneven steps. *You're working miracles.* You might not be recognized for it, but you are.

Showing up every day and working toward your vision as you meet the diverse needs of every student in your care is enough. You are enough. Your students are enough. Learning is a lifelong process, and we all get better with time and experience.

Push through the learning curve and don't let failures stop you

As you take on the risk of innovating and plan ways to adapt to all the changes in our field, be prepared for some things you try to be unsuccessful. Since all adventures involve risk and an uncertain outcome, that means they also involve the possibility of failure.

Don't become convinced that a single ineffective lesson is going to cause your students to fail the test and you to lose your job. You can never enjoy teaching if that's your perspective. Expect failure. Plan for it. Take away its power to catch you off guard. Woody Allen said, "If you're not failing every now and then, it's a sign you're not doing anything very innovative."

It's *good* for your students to see your mistakes and how you learn from them. Model for kids how to embrace unexpected change and new challenges. Lead by example as you show them how to rebound from failures and learn from the things that didn't go right.

Whenever our students encounter something that is difficult or frustrating, we always encourage them to push through it. We tell them to keep practicing and keep problem-solving, and eventually their efforts will be worth it. It's much more fun for us to play the role of "expert" in the classroom and not place ourselves in a position where we, too, have to keep working on something that's hard for us.

The constant changes in education keep us humble. They force us to stay in the position of a learner. And *that*, if nothing else about the situation, is a good thing.

Remember that every adventure involves something that is not fun

When I tell my mom about my travel and speaking schedule for the weeks ahead, she often responds by saying, "Whew. I don't know how you can stand to fly so much." I always smile and answer the same way: "Mom, I don't like flying. I like being in awesome places." For me, it's worth it to be uncomfortable for a little while in order to experience something really cool.

That's the way adventures go, don't they? You might have to travel a long way to get there. You might have to save up money for an adventure. You might be really, really tired afterward. *But these are all parts of the process that you endure because you want to get to the adventure.*

In teaching, you've got to endure the paperwork, testing, behavioral issues, meetings and all of that other stuff that isn't fun in order *to get to the adventure of seeing your students learn and grow.* You just have to buckle down and get through the rest, because you know on the other side of it is something that's worth all the effort and expense and inconvenience and discomfort.

Watching kids learn is one of the greatest adventures you'll ever have. You have the privilege of seeing light bulb moments on a daily basis. You get to see emotional breakthroughs that kids make, and watch them experience developmental milestones. You get to leave work each day knowing that there are children whose lives are better now than they were this morning, and kids who are smarter now than they were a few hours ago. At the end of your day's adventure in the classroom, you have the privilege of knowing there are kids who are becoming better readers, writers, mathematicians, scientists, and more...all because of the work that you chose to do.

Don't let the hard parts of teaching steal your sense of accomplishment and keep you from recognizing the magnitude of the job you're doing. Don't let fear of the unknown shake your confidence. We never know what's going to happen each day in the classroom, but that can be part of what makes teaching so fun!

Never be afraid to go on the adventure of helping kids learn and grow: your failures and theirs are an important part of the journey. Keep exercising your creativity and best judgment as an education professional. Keep innovating. Stay focused on the adventure that comes with outlasting the changes, adapting to them, and helping kids learn, no matter what.

It's not going to be easy. It's going to be *worth it*.

Get Connected

Are you ready for more great ideas and opportunities to connect with inspiring educators? Visit unshakeablebook.com to find links to all the resources you've just read about, and more!

About the Author

ANGELA WATSON was a dedicated classroom teacher for 11 years, and has turned her passion for helping other teachers into a career as an educational consultant. As founder of Due Season Press and Educational Services, she has published four books, launched three online courses, hosts a weekly podcast, designs curriculum support materials, provides instructional coaching services, and presents at conferences and schools around the world.

For more information about Angela (including professional development bookings), please visit TheCornerstoneForTeachers.com.

Notes

Notes